# Reinventing AGING

# Reinventing AGING

Shirley Yoder Brubaker,
Project Coordinator

Edited by Melodie M. Davis
Foreword by Justina Heese

**Herald
Press**

*Scottdale, Pennsylvania*
*Waterloo, Ontario*

**Library of Congress Cataloging-in-Publication Data**
Reinventing aging / Shirley Yoder Brubaker, project coordinator ; edited
by Melodie Davis ; foreword by Justina Heese.
    p. cm.
Includes bibliographical references.
ISBN 0-8361-9247-8 (pbk. : alk. paper)
1. Aging—Religious aspects—Christianity. 2. Aging—Social aspects.
I. Brubaker, Shirley Yoder. II. Davis, Melodie M., 1951-
BV4580.R445 2003
261.8'3426—dc21

                                                      2003004434

To our parents—the contributors

# Contents

# Foreword

*E*ver since I listened to the stories my grandmother told me as I sat at the edge of her bed, I have been intrigued with the wisdom and the worth of older adults. Even today this intrigue continues in my relationship with my parents who are in their early nineties. In spite of these powerful, positive relationships with older adults within my immediate family, the writers of *Reinventing Aging* identified many issues and feelings that I need to give further thought and consideration.

Each chapter of this book features a writer chosen because of a particular expertise on aging. Through vignettes and stories we are introduced to these writers as well as to the information they offer. This perhaps is the real genius of this book. The advice and expertise is presented within the context of the individual writer's life and experience, so each chapter provides another opportunity for the reader to identify with the aging process and to join the dialogue about aging. This format makes this book easy to adapt for study in a group setting.

Aging is a process in which all of us are chronologically, emotionally, and spiritually involved. Where we are in the process determines which information we will deem valuable and applicable to our lives. Each of the chapters of *Reinventing Aging* provides an opportunity to deal with the real issues facing the reader.

Providing specific information as some of the writers have is one of the strengths of this book. I found this specific guidance especially useful in the chapters on dying and funerals. At this same time, such chapters assume that readers will need to make appropriate legal and cultural adaptations if they reside in other states or countries.

I found the study questions and the exercises in the appendix of special value. Providing some structure can facilitate meaningful conversations for families and groups.

*Reinventing Aging* is an ambitious book with a commendable goal. Our society's largely negative portrayal of older adults is well entrenched. Whether this book will be able to revolutionize the way the readers will see and respond to older adults will in part be determined by the support and encouragement they will receive from their faith community. The study questions and activities make this book well suited to equip the faith community to provide the needed support.

*Justina Heese, Director*
*Christian Formation Council*
*Mennonite Church Canada*

# Preface

*T*he idea for this study curriculum on aging for people in their middle years began within the Health and Mutual Care Commission of Virginia Mennonite Conference. Because aging was an issue the commission wanted to address, they appointed a Subgroup on Aging to lead in that task.

The initial concern of the subgroup was how people are or are not planning to finance the possibility of nursing homecare in their future. As the group talked, it became clear that there were other aging issues that also needed to be addressed. Much has been written for the general public on issues related to aging, but the subgroup was surprised to discover that there were not many resources for the church. They believed discussions about preparing for aging should occur within the church family, as well as the family circle.

One of the subgroup members was the director of Virginia Mennonite Retirement Center, and at the March 2001 commission meeting, he suggested that the commission appoint a task force to prepare a curriculum on aging that could be used by Sunday school classes, small groups, and families.

The work of that task force is what you hold in your hands. When a task force member had expertise in an area, he or she wrote the appropriate chapter. Other chapters were written by people outside the task force who were experienced in a particular area.

This book was written for people who are still in the "denial years." Those are the years of the late forties, fifties, or early sixties and, of course, aging is years away, we think. But these are the very years when we should be preparing for how we want to live and be cared for when we are older.

Our hope as a task force is that you study this book with others from your church family. Rearrange the chapters to suit your interests, spending three weeks on one chapter or covering two chapters in one week. Invite guests to tell their stories or share their expertise. Take field trips. Above all, help each other acknowledge that the gift of still being alive means aging.

A video is available to accompany you on your journey through this study. The video segments introduce many of the chapters with some thought-provoking quote, anecdote, or interview. Discussion leaders should note the Leader's Guide (appendix A). There are study questions, activity suggestions, and resources, as well as more information on how to obtain and use the companion video. We also desired to make this study useful for intergenerational groups. Child-friendly activities are highlighted in the leader's guide, but all can be expanded or adapted for use when children are part of the group.

*Shirley Yoder Brubaker, Chair*
*Task Force on Aging Curriculum*
*Virginia Mennonite Conference*

# Acknowledgments

*T*his book had a lot of people contribute their knowledge, expertise, and experiences, which we gratefully acknowledge:

The Health and Mutual Care Commission of Virginia Mennonite Conference appointed a task force to create an educational curriculum on aging (primarily for baby boomers) that would bring growth, meaning, and understanding related to the tasks of growing older.

The Village at Morrisons Cove, a Church of the Brethren facility, participated in sponsoring this book by giving both staff time and money for its production.

Mennonite Publishing House agreed to publish the book portion and helped pay production expenses.

Virginia Mennonite Retirement Community contributed expertise and feedback at various points along the way.

Mennonite Mutual Aid contributed funding and feedback.

Mennonite Media, a department of Mennonite Mission Network, agreed to produce the video segments and contributed video expertise and production personnel.

The following people (some also wrote chapters) participated in the planning of this project: Shirley Yoder Brubaker, chair; Lonnie Yoder, Sheri Hartzler, Ann

Bender, Pearl Lantz, Beryl Brubaker, Ron Yoder, Keith Gnagey, Bob Neff, Owen Burkholder, Phyllis Liskey, Jill Landis, Kelli Burkholder King, James Horsch, and Burton Buller.

Shirley Yoder Brubaker, in chairing the task force, brought passion, pastoral expertise, personal experience, keen editing insights, along with wonderful administrative ability to see a job through.

Ron Yoder, president of Virginia Mennonite Retirement Community, a colleague from our mutual years of work with what was then Mennonite Board of Missions, approached me about this project. He told me I was going to be asked to serve as editor and compiler and urged me to take it on. While I was probably crazy to take it on apart from my other work, I have learned so much and it has made me aware of issues facing my own family. It has also served (I hope) as invaluable preparation for my own years when I will be older than I am now! I hope it will do the same for all who read or use it as it is intended, in a six-to-thirteen-week study with a small group or religious education class with a community of faith.

—*Melodie M. Davis, Editor*

# CHAPTER 1

# The Time of Our Lives

By Melodie M. Davis

> It is a mistake to regard age as a downhill grade
> toward dissolution. The reverse is true. As one
> grows older, one climbs with surprising strides.
> —George Sand

*I* recently had the occasion to sit and eat with a woman I'll call Martha. She is in her eighties, has increasing blindness, and also has great difficulty walking due to ongoing hip and knee problems. She had hip replacement surgery and gets around with a cane.

All her life Martha has been very active, working, volunteering, and traveling. She and her husband enjoyed a good income but were also very generous, giving of their time, as well as their money. So I could hear the wistfulness coming through when I asked how she was doing. She can no longer quilt, read, or do much of anything with her hands because of failing eyesight.

"Well, I'm *almost* getting to the place where I can sit and do nothing. Almost. I don't like it, but I can almost do it." Then she added, "Losing my eyesight—that's hard. It is hard to give up driving. We can't really travel by air, either. I really miss that. This morning my kids are flying to California. I envy them."

### Attitude

The time of our lives? Who are we trying to kid? Can the last part of life be the best part, or, as the poet Robert Browning wrote in "Rabbi Ben Ezra," "Grow old along with me! The best is yet to be, the last of life, for which the first was made."

Even earlier than Browning, the writer of Proverbs penned, "Wisdom is a tree of life to those who embrace her. Happy are those who hold her tightly."

I had my fiftieth birthday last December and sure enough, a month or two later, the dreaded invitation from the American Association of Retired Persons arrived in the mail. Okay, so I didn't send in my membership card. I had been warned that the AARP mailing would be a definite sign that I was truly over the hill. Shortly before that birthday I got involved working on this study book on aging. So I am squarely in the generation for whom this study is primarily intended.

I'm learning that as with every stage of life, getting older has as much to do with attitude as age. In parenting, if you anticipate that the two's will be terrible, they'll be terrible; if you dread the teenage years, they'll be dreadful. The same is true of the sixties and beyond. Some of our attitudes create self-fulfilling prophecies. "Aging is what you make it," several senior citizens remarked at a breakfast meeting. Of course, illness and accidents bring misery at any age.

There is something in us, though, that makes us wish we didn't have to look at this topic. You may think you're too young for a class on it. When it comes to aging, most of us are in massive denial. That doesn't mean if we try to stay fit, healthy, and active that we are in denial. My fifty-five-year-old sister informed me that likely I'll put off getting the AARP card for a year or two, and then the time will come when I'm glad to get the discounts. "Try selling products or raising money for programs that use the word aging," say Thomas R. Cole and Barbara Thompson, editors of a special edition of *Generations,* the journal of the American Society on Aging. "Growing old has never been fashionable in the country of the young."

But if you keep on with this book and topic (if you are studying it as a group) we can guarantee you one thing: while you may find out some things you won't like about the road ahead, we hope you'll discover that indeed this can be a great time of life. It's nice to know what may be in the future—it takes away some of the anxiety. It's like checking a road map before you launch a trip.

I'm fortunate to be part of the baby boom generation (and I like to think I'm at the tail end of it, of course). The baby boomers, because of their sheer numbers, are creating new waves as with all the other ages we encountered. Some of the waves are unnerving, like how will so many be supported by so few on "old age" government programs. Other changes are more encouraging, such as the stereotypes about aging that will be altered or vanish as baby boomers challenge those expectations.

Experts say the baby boom generation will cause all kinds of changes. Ira Byock, a medical doctor and author of the book, *Dying Well,* refers to "the coming tsunami of caregiving." Eve Harold, author of *I'll Be There: Caring For Your Parents, Job, and Marriage,* calls it a seismic shift, changing how goods, services, and money will be distributed, and not just in North America. A demographer for the United Nations' population division, Joseph Chamie, notes that "the world's population is steadily getting older everywhere." Predictions are that by 2050 there will be four working-age people in the world for every person over sixty-five. (In 1950, the ratio was twelve to one. In 2000, it was nine to one.)

One of the more subtle difficulties regarding aging is

the identity issue. I have heard elderly people say they are asked frequently, "And who did you used to be?" meaning, of course, "What did you used to do?"

"Well, I used to be a pastor, but I'm still Moses Slabaugh," is how one older gentleman responded to this query. This loss of identity can become a faith struggle: Did I lose my identity with my job? Who am I? What am I to do now? The elder years become as much of a struggle with identity as the classic struggles of the adolescent years. This can provide a linkage between the generations, knowing we struggle with the same things.

There are gender differences in how people age; generally women get their feelings out in the open while men may be more apt to brood and become depressed.

Most older people experience a serious learning curve entering this stage of life: life is different. If you retire at sixty-five and live until you're ninety-five (which is not that unusual), you have almost a third of your life left. Some folks working in the field of aging refer to this as the "third age vocation." Oftentimes the messages given to retirees are "You need to conserve, rest, and sit by." These are all very counterproductive. Are you going to just throw away a third of your life? While the middle aged generation is totally stressed out and busy, why should the elderly sit by? Programs linking older, middle aged, and younger bring benefits to all.

### Problems balance with benefits

There are serious problems during the older years. Since we live near my husband's relatives, most of my recent experiences with elderly people have been through his family; they've taught me a lot not only about aging, but living.

We went to visit an elderly aunt. She had no appetite and was wasting away. We all worried about her, urging her to eat, bringing her milkshakes, fried chicken, and all her favorites. Frequently she would push everything away and say, "I'm *never* hungry."

One day I responded, "That's funny," meaning, "That seems so strange."

This aunt retorted, "That's *not* funny!" and I had to realize, she's right. Losing your appetite is not funny or a blessing or anything else we who struggle with weight might think it to be. It is scary and life threatening. While her situation was made worse because of an operation she'd had, other senior citizens have told me that appetites change with increasing age. A juicy pork chop doesn't even sound good, they said. Food doesn't taste or look the same.

Another time this aunt's meal tray arrived and she just looked at it. I started cutting the food and tried to put it in her mouth. "I want to feed myself!" she managed to say. I was embarrassed. Of course she wanted to be as independent as possible.

Then there is the problem of battling changes in mind, memory, and mental alertness. My grandmother and grandfather lived in small quarters adjoining our home, so I was very fortunate to have that blessing during the first fourteen years of my life. Really it was ideal: they had their own separate living quarters, so they and we had privacy.

But I remember Grandma's growing confusion as she aged. I remember her continual worrying over the "gypsies" that were camped up in the woods. My father actually drove to the woods on the adjoining property to check out whether anyone was camping out in the woods, just to reassure her. He would tell her over and over that there weren't any gypsies up there, that he had gone and checked.

I have watched as friends at church, in the neighborhood, and family struggle with the increasing and encroaching indignities of aging. One vivid picture in my mind is of a very refined elderly woman, a friend of ours. Her first indignity came, she said, when she had to have a bowel movement on a porta-stool in the middle of her hospital room, rather than in the seclusion of a bathroom. She said suddenly she became aware that the door to her room was completely open during this private moment. Her next indignity came when her need to use the bathroom was so urgent she had to ask her visitors to step out, because she knew she couldn't control the urge. Finally, one night she lay wet in bed all night, being too chagrined to bring it to the attention of a nurse. Her experiences made me hurt and worry about the future.

But anyone at any age can testify to the loss of privacy that one experiences when ill or in the hospital. This is not just a problem or issue for the aged.

Other problems people experience: Erma was in her eighties. After her husband had a stroke, they lived in a retirement apartment, and she struggled to keep their financial books, which was something her husband always did. She struggled with being patient with her husband—such as when he tried to help her make the bed. He just couldn't smooth it out like she wanted, even though he wanted to do it. It wasn't in him. So she found that frustrating. She said that even though there were people all around her in the retirement home, she felt she really couldn't share deeply with them.

Lois told how her husband retired first and wasn't very busy. This was a major source of frustration for them since she was still running a part-time business from their home. He tried to help out by doing the housework, which he had never done much of. "I finally got up the nerve to tell him he didn't have to fold my underwear," Lois said. "They didn't fit in the drawer the way he folded them. He also folded the towels wrong; they wouldn't fit in the cupboard. These are such little things, but it is symbolic of all the changed roles of retirement," Lois added.

Another woman in her nineties told how even having meals in the retirement center became a source of anxiety. She was gradually losing control of her elimination system, and she was terribly afraid of having an attack of diarrhea while in the dining room. "One lady would have me out of here if I had an accident in the dining room," Beatrice confided. She said she usually went to the dining room an hour early to avoid sitting with those who made her nervous; if she was nervous, she had trouble eating. Fortunately, the nurses allowed her to eat in her room.

### Combating stereotypes

One of my husband's aunts told me recently, "Don't ever get old, Melodie. Aging is not fun."

After I wrote this statement about aging in my "Another Way" newspaper column, Rhoda Cressman, a reader in Pennsylvania, wrote to me about the column. She said she spends her time, at sixty-nine, on a forty-acre farm growing trees, wildflower and bird-nesting meadows, berry patches, orchards, and gardens (as well as pursuing many other interests), and wanted to amend that line above to say, "*Illness* is not fun, no matter what the age." And that is very true. It is illness and other symptoms that cause us problems, not age. She goes on, "I know lots of advanced-age folks who are fairly healthy, have equanimity, wonderful humor, positive attitude, excitement and interest in life, and rewarding interaction with other people." This kind of aging *is* fun.

She pointed me to a quote by George Sand: "It is a mistake to regard age as a downhill grade toward dissolution. The reverse is true. As one grows older, one climbs with surprising strides."

Cressman writes of the benefits of age: "What about

the insights, the greater ability to see what's important, the values and priorities being clearer, greater tolerance and mellowness, a greater capacity for love, patience, and compassion? Our culture focuses too much on the losses and not enough on the gains. There's another side to growing older than just the changes in the physical body."

Cressman attempts to battle stereotypes on aging wherever she encounters them. She dislikes comments like "Age is a very high price to pay for maturity." It may be funny, but she rewrites it to say, "Maturity is one of the rewards of old age." (But don't count her as humorless: she recognizes that the first statement is funnier.)

And I liked her take on the currently popular phrase used whenever someone is forgetful, having a "senior moment." She has decided that whenever she hears someone over fifty say something wise, insightful, helpful, or profound, she will say with an affirming smile, "Hey, I do believe you're having a senior moment!"

Sylvia Simmons, writing the "My Turn" column in *Newsweek,* told how she had received a card from the lieutenant governor of her state wishing her a happy birthday and telling her she could now enjoy "a life filled with cherished memories."

"That card infuriated me. I do not plan to spend the rest of my days looking backward," Simmons wrote. She had once been a Peace Corp worker, as well as a volunteer with the Red Cross during World War II, and has traveled to wonderful places all around the world. Yet there were plenty of things she still wanted to do—creating more memories, not just cherishing old ones.

### Aging as one part of life
Aging is part of life. To try to avoid aging is to rob life of some of its beauty. That's not to say that everything about aging is beautiful, as we have seen. It can be

painful—physically and emotionally. Those who work in the field of aging say there are three keys to aging successfully: 1) continue your education, continue to learn; 2) continue to develop relationships; and 3) continue to be involved in the community.

Barbara Thompson, a professor at the Institute for Medical Humanities, Galveston, Texas, has concerns about some of the anti-aging medicine that is appearing. "I worry that in our quest for continuing youth, we are perhaps not keeping . . . aging in perspective. As I talk to many of my older patients, I see the serenity they have and the long-range view. Aging offers opportunities to become more fulfilled as human beings." She feels that by embracing aging, we rise above the indignities, pain, and frailties.

My aunt Susie had a wry sense of humor and she taught my family many things about aging well. As she neared death she seemed to go back and forth between the actual world, the world in her mind, and the future world of heaven that she believed in passionately. We never knew what "world" we would find her in when we went to visit. She would talk about "eating cookies under the kitchen table with Jesus" and I thought, "She is just thinking so much about heaven she is imagining she is there."

She was particularly confused after one surgery, which had been intended to make her more comfortable. I'm told that anesthesia often makes elderly patients quite confused for up to six months or more after the surgery.

One day after surgery, her pastor, John Murray, came to see her. He and everyone thought that her life was surely nearing the end. He walked in and thought she was asleep. But he put his hand on her shoulder and said, "Susie, it's John Murray here to see you." Susie opened her eyes, quickly grabbed his arm with both hands and with surprising strength, pulled him down to where his face was directly in front of hers. She said, "John Murray, if you're here, I must not be dead yet." He said he didn't know what he did to keep from laughing out loud, but that he assured her that she was still very much alive.

Susie went on to live several more years and John continued to visit her. One day she had been looking at her church's bulletin. When John arrived, she counseled her pastor: "You are just too busy. I want you to sit in that chair and rest a while." John did as he was told.

Shortly before she celebrated her one hundredth birthday, he wrote, "It is a gift to be able to walk with people like Susie in the later stages of life. Susie's example has shown me what it means to be faithful in life and to live in faith at the end of life. She has shown me that I don't need to fear either nursing homes or death, and that our spirit and God's spirit continue in communion even when our minds have become clouded."

And that's what most of us want, isn't it? To not fear aging or death. The psalmist gives a beautiful description related to old age: "The righteous will flourish like a palm tree, they will grow like a cedar of Lebanon; planted in the house of the Lord, they will flourish in the courts of our God. They will still bear fruit in old age, they will stay fresh and green, proclaiming, 'The Lord is upright; he is my Rock, and there is no wickedness in him'" (Psalms 92:12-15).

The Bible is full of examples of age bringing wisdom to youth. In Exodus 18:3-24, after Moses (and God) got the Israelites out of Egypt, Jethro checks in with Moses, who tells him all about the plagues and the miraculous escape. Then Moses takes his seat as judge for all the people. People stand around him from morning until evening and he helps them settle disputes.

Wise old Jethro worries about this workload for his son-in-law (like Aunt Susie worrying about her pastor), and tells him he'll burn out. He suggests Moses delegate some of the cases to other judges, who will only bring the most difficult cases to Moses (see verse 22). One could argue that Jethro set in place the system of lower courts and higher courts we still use today—a pretty profound plan if you happen to be the first person to ever think of it. So the older generation imparts good sense and wisdom to the next (and succeeding!) generations.

# CHAPTER 2

# What Happens as We Grow Old: The Developmental Tasks of Aging

By Lonnie Yoder

> Old age is something everybody else reaches
> before we do.
> —Unknown

During a sabbatical year in Jamaica (2001-2002), I was introducing Chris, a young and relatively new Jamaican Mennonite pastor, to three of the Mennonite churches on the Santa Cruz Mountain. As we drove toward the first of the churches, Chris indicated that we would be passing near a small, rural Berean Church of God where he had served several years before in an internship while completing his Bible school degree.

We took a slight detour on our journey and I was fortunate to meet and spend about two hours with Sister Green, a woman in her late seventies and a lay leader of the church. As we drove down a red dirt Jamaican lane to a farmhouse and farm, Chris speculated about how he would be received by Sister Green after no contact over the past two years. No sooner had we arrived than Sister Green, who looked to be in her late fifties rather than seventies, embraced Chris with a passion and swung him around and around exclaiming that "her Chris" had returned.

Chris exclaimed, "Woman, where do you get your power? You are strong, woman!" Over the course of our visit Sister Green (also known affectionately as "Mummie Green" by the church members) showed us her considerable farming operation that involved the raising of numerous vegetables, showed us the new addition to the church building, and ushered us around the small, close-knit, rural community.

Sister Green was not only strong physically, but also acutely adept socially and spiritually. She had recently spearheaded the doubling in size of the church building by combining simple community fundraising with hands-on construction by the fifteen women who comprised the core of the church. She also coordinated the programs and ministry of the church in a healthy and wholesome manner. She took great pride in telling us that they "don't fuss" in their church; that is, they deal with conflict in a reasonable and sensitive manner. Sister Green commented on the state of the community and the church with both insight and foresight. As we left, she prophesied that she would live to see the completion of the church expansion project, and then she would be ready to die! Sister Green, a woman full of life but willing to acknowledge the inevitability of death, had been our teacher on that warm spring day high in the Santa Cruz Mountain of Jamaica.

### Myths about aging

Sister Green exemplifies a vibrant, yet realistic, picture of aging. However, we have to admit that her experience is probably not the norm. There are many ways that people both anticipate and experience aging. Whatever our culture or whatever our experience, we bring certain assumptions to the process and experience of aging. For many in North America, old age is a time to be postponed and avoided if possible, a less-than-desirable time in the lifecycle. Some people view old age as a time to shift into neutral—a time to be rewarded for a life of hard work. Still others view old age as a time of multiple and significant losses including the possible loss of career, spouse, peers, freedom, independence, and power. Most of these assumptions reveal what we now call "ageism," a denial of death and a bias toward the new and young. And this phenomenon flies in the face of the reality that we have an ever-increasing aging population in most countries of the world.

As a result of ageism, we are constantly faced with certain myths about aging. Ken Dychtwald and Joe Flower identify six such myths in their book, *Age Wave: The Challenge and Opportunities of an Aging America*. These six myths are:
> –People over sixty-five are old.
> –Most older people are in poor health.
> –Older minds are not as bright as young minds.
> –Older people are unproductive.
> –Older people are unattractive and sexless.
> –All older people are pretty much the same.

Some other myths that could be added to this list include:
> –Most older people have no family and live alone.
> –Most old people live in an institutional setting.
> –Most old people are poor.

You can probably think of other myths.

Why, we might ask, do we have such problematic views toward aging and quickly accept myths that portray aging in a negative manner? Perhaps we need look no further than the underlying framework that we bring to the process of aging. For many years the predominant model of aging has been one which views aging as a process of decline, disengagement, and loss. In other words, it is a time to be put out to pasture. In a 1998 editorial in the journal *America*, three primary models of aging are identified:

**1. The deficiency model.** This model, like the one identified above, focuses on the decline and loss that comes with aging.

**2. The consumption model.** This model encourages the aging person to have fun, travel, and seek reward for the life lived to that point.

**3. The wisdom model.** This model draws on a gift often present with aging, namely wisdom, which can be used in the interchange and relationship with those who are in younger generations. This model points us in the direction of a more wholesome view of aging.

A balanced model of aging views it as a process of growth, engagement, and integration that incorporates both loss and gain. This view accentuates the positive opportunities and challenges of aging, but also acknowledges the sometimes-harsh realities that come our way as we age. Overall, this view sees aging as a series of developmental tasks or challenges that we must engage to age well.

Before we look at these developmental tasks, it is appropriate to acknowledge that aging involves multiple losses. First, there are clearly physical losses that we may encounter as we age, such as losing part or all of our hearing or sight. We also lose significant social roles that we may have filled for a long time in our lives. The most obvious of these losses comes with our shift from being a full-time wage earner to a person who becomes primarily a consumer economically. If we live long enough, we all begin to lose our independence and mobility. This is most clearly symbolized by the loss of our driver's license at some point in life. Perhaps most significant is the loss of meaningful people and relationships in our lives. The death of a spouse or of a close friend or companion represents no small challenge as we seek to adjust. These are only a few of the losses that occur. Given these multiple and significant losses, how can we view aging as a time of growth, engagement, and integration?

We must also acknowledge the presence of certain gains as we age. David Wolfe, in his book *Serving the Ageless Market,* divides adulthood into three experiential stages:

**1. Possession experiences.** First is the stage where we work at establishing our adult identity. This often involves some form of productiveness, whether that is through our work, our family life, or some other way in which we find meaning and contribute to something larger than ourselves.

**2. Centered experiences.** Second, Wolfe argues that we enter a stage of centered experiences where we simply enjoy our adult identities and focus more on purchasing services than things.

**3. Being experiences.** Finally, in the latter part of life, he contends that we enter a stage where we recognize our connection with all of humanity and focus on questions and issues of meaning in more deliberate ways. This stage often involves going back to previous experiences and places in our lives to integrate them into this stage.

For example, one may return to the scene of one's childhood—the family farm or an apartment in the city—in order to incorporate this part of our life into one's present experience. This stage also involves enjoying the simple but profound realities in life, such as a beautiful sunset. Wolfe cites a survey in which people were asked whether they had watched a sunset in the past month. In the survey only two people under the age of fifty had done so. Fifteen people over the age of fifty had done so.

I once heard an older person say that "you move from a curriculum of required courses to elective courses" as you age. This is a creative way of saying that aging often brings new freedoms and new opportunities that contribute to the possibility of growth in one's life. Time may take on new meaning for us, becoming our ally rather than our foe. There may be self-esteem gains as well. If we age well, we may discover that we enjoy simply "being" as much, or even more, than all the "doing" that we have been involved in during our previous years. Aging also opens the possibility of spiritual growth and integration. Some people discover a spiritual depth in their later years that eluded them in earlier stages of life.

The gospel of Luke provides a wonderful example of how two biblical characters aged in a wholesome manner. We find them both in the account of Jesus' presentation at the temple by his parents (Luke 2:22-38). First, Simeon, a righteous and devout man who clearly possessed the Holy Spirit, is guided to the temple, where he holds the baby Jesus and prophesies about Jesus' central role in the salvation of all peoples. Simeon blesses both the child Jesus and his parents—a wonderful example of intergenerational exchange. Then, Anna, the prophetess, enters the scene and also highlights the central role that Jesus will play in God's redemption plan. Note that Anna, a woman widowed at a young age, met that loss by finding a new role of prayer and fasting in the temple. She, too, in her simple act of praise and confirmation, blesses Jesus and his parents. Both Simeon and Anna model a way of aging which involves growth, engagement, and integration.

### Developmental tasks of aging

There are a series of developmental tasks that can guide us in our process of growth, engagement, and integration.

**1. Responding to change both in the form of loss and gain.** As we have already noted, there are multiple losses that come with aging. The prophetess Anna represents one of those—the loss of a spouse. How did she successfully deal with this loss? The Scriptures do not tell us, but we can surmise what might have contributed to her wholesome move into a new sense of vocation and relationship in her life. First, she must have been able to grieve well the loss of her husband. The capacity to grieve well will help us deal with the multiple losses that come our way in aging. This is something that we can practice from a very early age. We all experience multiple losses every year of our lives. These often come in the form of what we could call "little losses." How do we incorporate the numerous little (and not so little) transitions and changes that accompany a simple move from one home to another? How do we grieve the loss of significant neighbors? Or how do we grieve the loss of a familiar and special view out one of our windows?

We choose, consciously or not, to respond to these losses every day of our lives. Let these "little losses" be our teachers as we prepare for the more significant losses that will inevitably come our way as we grow old.

Stress reduction and need satisfaction are two other ways we can deal with losses that come our way. One way we can do this is to increase the amount of control that we have in a given situation. Rather than focusing on loss of control in some form, we can find ways to maximize our sense of control in other areas. Studies have shown that simply having a plant or pet to care for can increase the sense of control and well-being of an aging person.

Finally, as we age we must become aware of the gains that come with aging and maximize them in our day-to-day life. New freedoms, for example, can be squandered or they can be incorporated into our lives in a way that enriches our experience. A sunset missed in our older years is no different than a sunset missed in our younger years.

**2. Developing new uses of time.** Time is a major stressor for most of us in our adult years. We never seem to have enough of it to fulfill our obligations and do all that we want to do. Our senior years often bring with them discretionary time. Some find this time to be a blessing and others find it more of a curse. Creatively choosing to invest our new-found time is a commendable challenge and goal. Some will find activities like gardening, volunteering, and simply "tinkering and puttering" to be of meaning as we age. More time to invest in personal relationships can also be a blessing. The challenge with respect to time involves being able to accept the different pace of life and to learn from it. We need to seek out opportunities that will enhance our lives and the lives of others. Spiritual growth is one commendable way to utilize the time that comes our way in the senior years.

**3. Developing new uses of space.** A major question all of us must address as we age is: Where will I grow old? I recall watching and walking alongside my great uncle Wally, who retired at the age of sixty-one and sold his home in the suburb and moved into a cottage in the local retirement community. He held his first auction at that time and reduced his earthly possessions in a significant manner. Then six years later he held yet another auction when he moved into a single room in the nursing area of the retirement community. Finally, he moved from one level of care in the nursing unit to another and was required to divest still more of his earthly possessions. He did this gracefully and in a way that had significant meaning for him. For example, he gave some of his possessions to a local historical museum and others to younger family members. I was encouraged and blessed as I watched him creatively negotiate the task of having less and less space in which to live.

**4. Integrating life experience.** Erik Erikson captured his eighth and final stage of growth in the challenge he called "ego integrity versus despair." He argued that some people reach old age and are able to say, "I have lived a good, but not perfect, life. Yes, I have made mistakes. But for the most part, I have lived a good life and I feel good about how I have dealt with all that has come my way." This state he named "ego integrity." For a person to be able to take this approach to the end of his or her life, some significant degree of integration has to have taken place. This often involves sustained reminiscing about what has happened in one's life. Helping one another reminisce is a valuable way in which we can grow in our senior years.

On the other hand, some reach the end of life and conclude, "Life is almost over and I basically blew it. I wish I had done many things differently." This attitude (Erikson called this state "despair") presents more of a challenge but is not beyond redemption. Reminiscing in this case may involve significant grieving of those things one has missed out on in life. Grieving may also occur over poor decisions one has made. In either case, reminiscing is a wonderful way to pass on experiences, values, and traditions to the next generations. It is a meaningful way to share one's wisdom with the next generations. It is also a way to begin to work at the "unfinished business" in one's life.

**5. Living in a dying way.** Inevitably and eventually, we will all have to face the reality of death. We will need to engage in a process of dying, whether that be long or short. Denial of this reality is not to our advantage even though our society gives us many opportunities to embrace that denial. It is important that we accept dying and death as an integral part of our life experience. In the story of Sister Green at the beginning of this chapter, you will recall that in spite of her robust approach to life in her late seventies, she was conscious of her impending death and willing to factor that into her framework and choices. We need to be sensitive to the developmental challenges that come with dying and death. In many ways, it is "the big loss" for which hopefully all of the preceding "little and not-so-little losses" have prepared us well.

Aging is not a simple nor lock-step process. We all age differently and must acknowledge the multiple ways in which we move through the final stages of life. Even for a given individual the aging process may vary depending on which area of life is being examined. For example, your chronological age may be one thing, while your physical-biological age, your psychological-mental age, your social-relational age, and your spiritual age may all be different. Also, with the increasing lifespan, scholars have begun to identify stages within the final stage of life. One model of these stages uses the following catchy phrases: the "go-go" stage, the "go-slow" stage, the "slow-go" stage, the "slow-slow" stage, and finally the "no-go" stage. The presence of these multiple stages means that we need to identify where in the aging journey a given person is in order to helpfully understand the respective developmental tasks and challenges the person may be facing.

There are clearly more challenges than the five developmental tasks we have listed above. But this list of five captures a significant portion of those challenges we will face. Like Sister Green, let us find ways to truly engage life while acknowledging the reality of multiple losses and eventually even death. Like Simeon and Anna of old, let us find ways to grow, engage, and integrate as we thereby encourage and bless the generations to come.

# CHAPTER 3

# What the Body Says: The Physical Aspects of the "Golden Years"

By Evelyn Driver

> Our culture focuses too much on the losses of aging and not enough on the gains. There's another side to growing older than just the changes in the physical body.
> —Rhoda Cressman

*I*t is graduation weekend at the university. The formal academic recognitions are complete, degrees and honors awarded. Now is the time to celebrate with family and friends. Several graduates have combined their friends and resources for one large event.

The twenty-somethings sit on the grass, eating highly spiced vegetarian culinary experiments and jump up at times to run and eagerly greet newly arriving guests. The forty- and fifty-somethings dutifully keep the table supplied with food and discuss the calorie, fat, calcium, and fiber content of the assorted casseroles and tempting desserts. Several women compare notes about bone density studies and the most recent theories with respect to hormone replacement therapy. The sixty- and seventy-something grandparents are present. Even the widowed eighty- and ninety-something grandparents are involved, although one is present while another is confined at home with a paid, nonfamily caregiver so all the family could attend the events.

One grandparent carefully surveys the available seats with an eye on the one "just right" chair of sufficient height to safely protect a newly replaced hip. Another moves to secure a seat in the warm sun away from the stiff wind that is blowing. All grandparents wait patiently for the crowd to clear from around the food tables—then examine the edible options with an eye for familiar favorites and low-sodium selections.

The sixty-somethings with thinning, salt-and-pepper hair quietly blend into the grouping of those a decade or so younger. One politely declines the coffee, with a comment that the caffeine will keep him awake. His older brother gives a quick agreement although fully recognizing the excuse as a probable cover for the real reason—to decrease the number of trips to the bathroom for small-volume urinary results.

A seventy-something smiles knowingly as she sees a fifty-something arise from a chair and take a moment to stretch a hip joint before walking confidently from the room. Two fifty-somethings discuss the joint and muscle consequences of the lengthy road trip required to reach the event.

What are the factors that represent normal aging differences, chronic disease effects, or simply personal preferences and habits? Several key concepts provide the foundation for this chapter. Use these as reminders as you read about changes the body experiences as it ages.

### Body facts related to aging

**1. The human body functions through the interaction of many systems.** No system can function alone. Change in any system affects other systems.

**2. Healthy body systems have reserve capacity that greatly exceeds the usual demands placed upon them** by active young adult people. Reserve capacity does decrease gradually over the decades. However, the body does have enough cells to function for an entire lifespan of even more than one hundred years.

**3. Many types of body cells are constantly being produced** to replace those that have been damaged or lost. For example, a red blood cell lives for approximately 120 days before being replaced by a newly produced one. Even the bones are living tissue and in a constant state of remodeling through a process intended to provide new bone cells at a rate equal to the normal rate of bone cell destruction.

**4. There is normally a gradual change in the function of body systems over the decades.** However, some changes that are evident among older adults are hard to separate from lifestyle and environmental effects on the human body. These changes can be difficult for the layperson to differentiate from chronic health problems. The longer a person lives, the greater their chances of developing some chronic health problem—but chronic health problems are *not* normal aging.

**5. People adapt to changes in function, some more effectively than others.** Normal changes are subtle and progressive. Although some experts claim that aging starts at birth, we typically make comparisons with the characteristics and function of the physical body at some "ideal" age, commonly the young adult years. Such comparisons can hinder efforts to adapt effectively and make us good targets for marketers who promote products claiming to "slow down aging."

**6. Just as the physical body of a twenty-five-year-old is different from the body of a sixty-five-year-old,** so too the body of a healthy person at age sixty-five is quite different from that at age 105. Our views of "normal" and of "healthy" must be adjusted for age.

**7. It is difficult for experts in the field of aging to make definitive statements about normal age changes** and to separate such changes from chronic disease conditions. Such clarity requires that the same very large group of people would need to be studied throughout their lifetimes of eighty-five plus years. There are a number of national research studies in progress that are beginning to provide answers to some of our questions about normal aging, especially in very advanced old age.

**8. "Use it or lose it."** This saying does apply to some aspects of bodily function. Research studies on brain, cardiovascular, and muscle function support this time-honored expression. Such research findings add support to the common sense advice to stay physically active and mentally involved in life in order to "stay young."

### What people are we talking about?

As a society, we have come to consider age sixty-five as the start of "old age," at least with respect to healthcare and Social Security issues. The older adult population covers a range of years from age sixty-five to at least 105 (a total of at least forty years). Within this age range people are subdivided into three, sometimes four distinctly different groups: sixty-five to seventy-four years old, seventy-five to eighty-four, and eighty-five and above. Recently, books and journal authors are adding yet a fourth group: that of age one hundred and above. The centenarians are typically healthy people whom researchers are now studying to discover the secrets of long life. Within each of these age groupings there is wide variation in almost any characteristic that one wishes to study.

The "average" life expectancy for humans has increased since the 1900s, primarily because of improvements in sanitation, control of communicable diseases with use of vaccines, development of antibiotics, and the more recent uses of technology. Consequently, those who reach age sixty-five today have a projected remaining life expectancy of thirteen to twenty years (depending on race and gender). Even at age eighty-five, remaining life expectancy is commonly cited as five to six and a half years.

Aging experts and researchers debate the various theories about the process of aging, each focusing on a preferred view by which to explain how cells and body structures eventually show the effects of aging. Each different theory has the potential to provide a basis for some "new treatment" for some of these effects. Currently research focused on the role of genetics in the aging process is gaining media attention.

Aging is a normal process. It is *not* a disease state. As a healthy mature person ages, he or she will experience a gradual decrease of cells, alterations in function, and changes that are apparent to others. Aging does not take place as a series of specific, discrete steps that can be objectively measured and marked off as "completed." As a person continues to live and function over time he or she may not be aware of the aging process. The changes are subtle, progressive, and usually the person is able to adapt to the changes. We notice changes in others at times such as the thirty or forty-year high school class reunion—and may begin to reflect on changes within ourselves.

We are all familiar with the stereotype of an older adult—all those physical characteristics that drive the marketing of products to forty- and fifty-somethings to preserve a youthful appearance. But aside from expenditures of time and money in a futile effort to turn back the clock, what are the changes that affect how we function within our circle of friends?

## Visual features

When you first meet another person, there are visual features that create a picture of who that person is. Let us follow two older adults who meet for the first time (perhaps during that graduation party detailed at the start of this chapter). The visual cues upon meeting someone new typically allow these two people to guess an approximate age, or at least the decade of life. They share the following characteristics with the newly found friend. Total body height is decreased because of loss of size of the spaces between the vertebrae (backbones) protecting the spinal column. Posture may become slightly stooped, and even more so in the presence of chronic disease processes such as osteoporosis of the spine and some neurological conditions.

Hair grows more slowly and gradually becomes gray. Thinning of the hair affects both males and females. Skin texture changes with thinning of the skin and loss of subcutaneous fat, all leading to wrinkles. Skin dryness becomes noticeable and calls for added attention to the types of skin care products used. There is a decrease in production of sweat, as well as slowed hair and nail growth. Nails become drier and break more easily. The ability to perceive touch, temperature, and vibration through the skin is decreased and can lead to an increased risk of injury.

The two new friends begin to communicate. This assumes thinking and language ability along with vision and hearing. Several normal age changes can create communication problems for older adults unless they adopt specific strategies to compensate for the changes.

## Vision changes

Vision changes begin to become apparent in the forties in the well-recognized "long-arm syndrome," as in the holding of the hymnbook at an increasing distance from the face. Later changes within the eye result in a scattering of light rays that produces problems dealing with glare from shiny surfaces. The pupil adapts more slowly to changes in light. There is a decrease in the ability to focus on closely held objects. Even the perception of colors such as blues and greens can be affected by certain changes within the eye. At night the glare from shiny objects, moisture, and oncoming traffic becomes troublesome and may adversely affect driving comfort and performance. Considerably more light is required for comfortable reading of printed materials. Bold print and contrasting colors are seen more easily than subtle shades and fancy script.

### Hearing changes

Hearing gradually changes over the decades due to several normal processes. Earwax accumulates more readily and may collect in the ear canal, obstructing sound waves. The tiny bones within the middle ear stiffen and conduct sound waves less efficiently. High-pitched sounds are harder to hear, and more time is required for the transmission of sound impulses along the nerves to the brain. An early indication that such changes are developing is the decreased ability to clearly hear words with the consonants *ch, f, g, s, sh, t, th,* and *z.* The problem is magnified if the speaker is talking rapidly, and worse if the voice is of a high pitch. Add to the mix of changes the presence of background noise or echoes within the room and the normal older adult is placed at a distinct disadvantage in social situations.

In addition to the normal age changes in hearing, older adults may have impaired hearing from accumulated damage to the ear from lifetime abuses. Notorious sources of damage include loud music, noisy work environments, motorcycle engines, tractors, chain saws, snow blowers, household appliances, and several types of medications. Men currently show more hearing impairment from noise than do women; however it is suggested that women are "catching up" as a result of equal job opportunities (and workplace noise exposure). The damage can be sufficient to change what would have been normal age changes into preventable hearing loss.

The two new friends shake hands to greet one another. Eye contact is important, but it can be difficult to see clearly at close range without tilting the head backward to use the "close-range portion" of the bifocals. They both smile and shake hands. The smile requires use of the intact neurological system. Muscles, joints, coordination, and touch all come into play.

### Movement

The new friends decide to go for a walk. The activity requires balance, muscle strength, intact bones, and an adequately functioning cardiovascular and respiratory system, each influenced by the neurological system's coordination of the process.

Bones are constantly being remodeled throughout life, but the rate at which this occurs and the balance between bone destruction and bone building is affected by aging as well as by lifestyle factors. Intake of nutrients such as calcium and the performance of weight-bearing exercise are among the essential factors needed for maintenance of optimum bone mass. The overall trend is toward bone loss with increasing age, placing the older person at increased risk of fractures with smaller amounts of trauma. Hip fractures are much-feared for the person with osteoporosis (thin bones). The fear can cause the person to become overly cautious, even limit their walking in the hope to decrease their risk of falls. This tendency usually increases the risk of falls because muscle strength is lost and the sense of balance is decreased when people decrease walking activities.

Joints gradually show wearing of the cartilage, though experts debate whether this is normal aging or the disease condition of degenerative joint disease (osteoarthritis). The soft tissues within the joints stiffen and become more likely to tear with sudden movements. There is less lubricant available for smooth joint movement. It becomes increasingly important for the older adult to do gentle warm-up and stretching exercises prior to performing major activities in order to decrease the risk of injury to muscles and ligaments. Actual destruction of joint surfaces severe enough to warrant joint replacement (hip or knee) is typically considered a disease process rather than normal aging.

### Cardiovascular changes

Over the decades, the large muscles of the arms and legs gradually decrease in size. This is associated with a gradual decrease in strength, endurance, and ability to function rapidly in a coordinated manner. The good news here is that specific exercises to promote strength and endurance can be useful in preserving the ability to move about and function safely and efficiently.

Cardiovascular system changes are subtle and complex. Gradual changes occur within the reflex mechanisms that control heart rate and blood pressure. The older adult needs to change position more slowly to decrease the risk of becoming dizzy upon standing. With exercise, the heart rate does not increase as much as expected in younger people. Target ranges for pulse rate must be age-adjusted. Following exercise, it takes longer for the older adult to recover and for the heart rate to return to the resting level. Properly planned exercise programs are considered beneficial, but experts disagree on the specific amounts and types of exercise that are recommended. Chest pain with exercise is not normal aging, and should be checked out by a healthcare provider.

### Respiratory system

The respiratory system also changes over the decades. Our new friends do not have colds or the flu so they do not need to worry about exposing one another to these respiratory infections. Normally the breathing system functions adequately even in advanced old age. However, with respiratory irritants and infections, such as a simple cold, added problems can develop and become more serious than in younger people. As we age, the small cells that help clear the bronchi of unwanted secretions and infections become less effective. The joints of the rib cage move less freely and shrinkage of the spinal column may decrease the amount of space in which the lungs can expand with deep breathing. Consequently, the older adult is at greater risk of developing complications such as pneumonia from minor upper respiratory infections. Once an infection is established, it takes longer for the older adult to recover.

### Eating

The couple stops by a restaurant. The association of eating with the gastrointestinal tract is obvious, but this system includes the grinding of food, swallowing, digestion, metabolism, and eventual excretion of the unused residual liquids and solids from that food. Each of these processes is affected by normal age changes.

Lifelong patterns of dental care become important to the maintenance of normal teeth and effective chewing. It is normal to experience gradual flattening of the cusps from years of use as well as hardening of the tooth enamel. Loss of teeth is *not* a normal age change in adult life.

While at the restaurant, the appreciation of the experience is affected by the senses of smell and taste, both of which can gradually decrease with age. The ability to detect salt and sugar in food may decrease and the older adult sometimes uses excessive amounts of these flavor enhancers. The older adult needs fewer calories because metabolism has gradually slowed over the decades. However, the amount of most nutrients needed remains the same or even increases with increased age. It becomes more of a challenge for the older adult to obtain meals with adequate nutrients while also limiting the calories, salt, and sugar in favorite foods.

There is a normal decrease in the amount of saliva, gastric secretions, and digestive enzymes that are produced. This can lead to stomach distress and can alter the way in which certain nutrients are absorbed from the digestive tract. The movement of food within the intestinal tract is slowed somewhat as a person ages and the person is more likely to develop constipation if dietary and activity modifications are not made.

### Elimination

As the evening progresses, fluids consumed with the meal have been converted by the kidneys to urine that is stored in the bladder. As the years pass, the bladder becomes less able to stretch and hold large volumes of urine. A smaller amount of urine in the bladder will produce a sensation of fullness. The strength of the small muscles that are surrounding the bladder outlet influence how well the flow of urine can be controlled. These weaken over the years, but specific exercises can help strengthen these muscles. For males, an enlarged prostate can cause problems emptying the bladder and result in more frequent trips to the toilet. Although there are changes in the volume of urine the bladder can hold, the leaking of urine is *not* normal aging and should be discussed with the healthcare provider.

### Brain changes

During the time at dinner, our two new friends begin to discuss brain changes associated with aging. Among middle age and older adults, one (perhaps the greatest?) fear is the development of "senile dementia" or Alzheimer's disease. They joke about "senior moments," claim "you can't teach an old dog new tricks," share stories of becoming alarmed when unable to immediately locate the car or house keys, and worry about times when that name is "on the tip of my tongue." They then attempt to validate their competency by giving younger people some "words of wisdom" and demonstrating how to do some clever, time-honored task.

There are some changes that occur in brain function in advanced age. The overall size and weight of the brain decreases slightly (10 percent spread from age twenty to age ninety). This is thought to be indicative of loss of brain cells. However, current thinking suggests that regeneration of brain cells also occurs, particularly when the older adult is regularly involved in mentally stimulating situations. Intellectual function that involves wisdom, creativity, judgment, common sense, and use of knowledge and experience does not decline and may even increase in the healthy older adult. Declines in brain function may be evident in the ability to fluently use words, to quickly comprehend verbal information, and to calculate numbers.

There are some normal changes in memory over the decades. Memory about specific events is more clear and accurate at age twenty than at age ninety. Short-term memory involving small bits of information does decline. There are specific strategies that older adults can (and often do) employ to compensate for this decline. Long-term memory is preserved, but accessing that large bank of stored data will take more time. A useful analogy is that of a computer with slower processing time. The data is preserved; it just takes longer to find all the pieces when the disk is getting full.

Memory for how to perform specific actions is generally retained. However, the actual performance of the task will likely be slowed because of changes in the speed with which impulses travel through the nerves. Older adults also tend to become more cautious in the performance of all activities, particularly if they suspect that someone is watching or evaluating their performance. Alzheimer's disease is *not* normal aging.

### Sexual function

If we were to follow this couple through the remainder of the their daily lives, changes to be addressed include sexual function, sleep quality, and temperature control. There are normal age changes that occur in each of these aspects of life.

The ability for sexual function is retained but altered for both women and men as the decades pass. For healthy older adults, the sex organs retain their ability to respond though the amount of lubrication and the intensity of the response decreases. The presence of chronic diseases such as diabetes and any disease affecting either the blood vessels or the nervous system is more likely to adversely affect sexual function than is aging alone. The ability to produce offspring diminishes and eventually ends for women by about age fifty. Men generally retain the ability to produce sperm into late life, but the amount produced decreases with age.

### Sleep patterns

Sleep changes are thought to occur with normal aging. In general the total amount of sleep within twenty-four hours remains about the same as in younger years. However, the total amount of time spent in bed *trying* to sleep is longer, mostly because it takes longer for the older adult to fall asleep. Once asleep there are changes in the quality of sleep and in the amount of time spent in the different stages of sleep. Less time is spent in the deepest stages of sleep with more time spent in the lighter stages. There is more waking during the night and it takes longer to return to sleep once the person is awakened. There may be a trip to the bathroom at night. However, if frequent trips are needed at night, the situation should be discussed with the doctor.

### Hot and cold

The ability of the body to regulate its temperature decreases over the decades and places the older adult at increased risk of ill effects from even moderate heat and cold. Cold environments can present problems because the reflex mechanisms and blood flow that help the body warm itself do not work as efficiently in advanced age. Hot environmental conditions can be particularly dangerous because the older adult is less able to sweat and thereby cool the body. There is a decrease in the ability of an older person to feel the sensations of environmental heat and cold. They may not be aware that they are having problems, or the effects of the heat or cold may make them unable to take appropriate actions to relieve the problem. In addition, inadequate fluid intake is common among older adults. The sense of thirst is not as reliable an indicator of dehydration in older adults. Special care is needed in hot weather to make sure an older person gets enough fluid even if the person does not feel thirsty.

### Summary

When we think about the aging of the physical body, two contrasting images can come to mind. One extreme is that everything wrinkles, sags, droops, dries up, and stops working, perhaps before the end of life on this earth. The other extreme is—if you follow all the correct recommendations of the latest proper health expert/ guru—you will forever maintain the appearance and function of the idealized "normal" twenty-five-year-old. Neither extreme accurately portrays the normal situation for a healthy older adult who moves from middle age into that brave new world of "old age." Somewhere between two extreme poles lies an individualized reality for each of us with respect to aging of the physical body. A useful analogy is that of a fine antique car that one intends to keep running for many years. With proper care and use, it can function well within the normal ranges expected for that vintage.

The psalmist provides us with a beautiful image of the aging person, even in the physical sense: "The righteous flourish like the palm tree, and grow like a cedar in Lebanon. They are planted in the house of the Lord; they flourish in the courts of our God. In old age they still produce fruit; they are always green and full of sap" (Psalms 92:12-14, NRSV).

"Full of sap!"? Hardly seems dried up or sagging at all. And no matter what our age or condition, it is useful to think in terms of "still producing fruit." (See also appendix C for a worship ritual for retirement using this verse and imagery.)

CHAPTER 4

# Body, Mind, Spirit: Personal Wellness

By Evelyn Driver

> It is magnificent to grow old if one keeps young
> while doing it.
> —Harry Emerson Fosdick

*A*lice has always been one of the mainstays of the congregation. For decades she has attended services regularly and used her many talents to contribute to the activities of church life. She is a tall, thin woman who has always given careful attention to her health, modified her driving habits to correspond to her normal age changes, followed a prudent diet, and enjoyed her interactions with her church family.

Now at age eighty-eight Alice has some trouble maintaining balance when standing and walking, but otherwise remains healthy. At church she has almost fallen several times because the children run freely in the aisles and lobby following the service. Even though they do not actually bump into her, simply the rapid movement within her field of vision makes it difficult for her to walk safely. Alice knows that a fall and broken hip for someone her age can be disastrous. She is about ready to stay home and worship by means of the tape ministry in order to maintain her physical health.

Maintaining wellness with advancing age cannot be viewed as simply a matter of personal attention to all the details of physical health maintenance. Two well-respected nurse specialists in the field of aging provide a useful background for the discussion of wellness in the later years of life. In their book, *Geriatric Nursing and Healthy Aging*, Priscilla Ebersole and Patricia Hess describe wellness as "achieving a balance between one's internal and external environment and one's spiritual, social, cultural, and physical processes." Within this use of the term, wellness includes physical health but goes beyond the physical to also include the emotional, mental, and spiritual dimensions. It also includes the concept of humans as living within a community.

In this chapter, personal wellness is viewed as a condition in which people are functioning at their optimum capacity even with advancing age. This involves both personal actions, as well as interactions within a community of people. It even includes attention to the function of social networks of which individuals are a part. Within communities, there is an implied responsibility to avoid creating unnecessary obstacles for others, particularly with respect to health and safety issues.

In one sense, the instructions for maintaining physical health as one ages can be summarized in one sentence: Continue to do all the common sense, healthy lifestyle activities that young adults should do, and make a few modifications to address some of the factors that present challenges for older adults. That sounds deceptively simple. Indeed, most of the needed actions are low-cost, readily available ones.

The common sense wisdom includes: eat your fruits and vegetables, get adequate sleep, balance work activity with recreation and rest, "let not the sun go down upon your wrath," and stay connected with others and with

God. This advice does not change simply because a person is "old." What does change is the physical body. These changes may call for modification in how one engages in these common sense activities. We are bombarded with many forms of information about ways to improve various aspects of healthy living. It seems that we are in an age of "health of the individual body part." Television and print media make appealing claims: Take Product X for eye health, take Product Y for colon health, take Product Z for bone health, etc. This leaves us either confused as to what actions to take, or with large expenditures of money if we yield to all the marketing claims. Individual body parts do not function in isolation and cannot each be kept young simply by taking the proper herb, medication, or dietary supplement. We all long for just the expert who can tell us exactly what we need to do to stay healthy and avoid all decline in any ability. Even if available, the information would need to be adapted to our own unique situations and would likely require changes in behavior. There are several areas in which age changes call for modifications in our lifestyle and habits as we age.

### Nutrition

Nutrition is one area in which each of us can usually exercise control. Gradual changes in the body call for changes in the amount of food consumed. Body metabolism slows gradually over the decades, so we need fewer calories to keep the body working. Those calories increasingly need to be ones that are "nutrient dense"—that have the needed nutrients without an excess of the calories and fat that are not needed. Additional attention needs to be directed toward decreasing the intake of salt and saturated fats while increasing fiber and calcium intake. For those who rely on purchased, prepackaged, heat-and-serve meals, additional attention should be given to reading of food labels, particularly to detect the amounts of salt, fat, and calories.

Attaining and maintaining ideal body weight can help control (perhaps even delay the onset of) some chronic disease conditions. These conditions include diabetes, high blood pressure, heart disease, and degenerative joint disease of the knees and hips. Nutrition *and* exercise play a role in weight control.

### Exercise

Exercise helps maintain the ability of the body to function. The adage "use it or lose it" is relevant particularly for maintaining function of bones, muscles, and joints. However, anyone who has been a couch potato for years must be sensible about the way in which he or she starts an exercise program. Start gradually and be realistic about what an out-of-shape fifty- or sixty-year-old body should try to do. Pay attention to signals from your body warning you to slow down. Don't try to compete with the twenty-year-old athletes (at least not initially). Walking is generally considered suitable exercise for anyone, but you should consult with your healthcare provider for specific details regarding types and amounts of other exercise appropriate for your situation. Some people find that exercising with a friend helps them stick with it.

As part of any exercise program, it is important to allow time to warm up and gently stretch the muscles to begin exercising. The session should end with a cool-down phase and gentle stretching of muscles. The older the person is, the more important this aspect of exercise becomes. If using heart rate as one of the ways of monitoring response to exercise, the calculation to find your target heart rate must be based on a formula that adjusts for advanced age.

## Sleep

Sleep in adequate amounts and of good quality is important to maintaining health. One common sleep problem for normal older adults can be difficulty falling asleep. Lifestyle modifications that may be helpful include avoiding caffeine in the late afternoon and evening and exercising during the daytime but not in the evening near bedtime. If you do not fall asleep shortly after going to bed, get out of bed and read or do some quiet activity until sleepy, then return to bed.

### Risk factors

Other aspects of maintaining health of the physical body include attention to the reduction of risk factors for specific illnesses (such as heart disease, cancer, diabetes) and following the advice of one's healthcare provider to be screened for early detection of treatable problems. Types of conditions to discuss include tests for colorectal cancer, prostate cancer, and breast cancer; bone density study to detect osteoporosis; and checking the amount of lipids (fats and cholesterol) in the blood. Using sunscreen when outside for reducing the risk of skin cancer, obtaining an annual influenza immunization (flu shot), and asking about a pneumonia vaccine can also be helpful in maintaining physical health.

The issue of maintaining wellness in the face of chronic limitations to physical function can be more complex. The issues may include the ways in which others see and respond to the person. Joe illustrates this situation with respect to age changes: that of the need to address self-concept and adapting to changes.

### Adapting to change

For years, Joe and his wife enjoyed their contacts and interactions with members of their congregation. Even since his wife died, Joe usually attends church and particularly likes listening to the messages. But Joe has trouble hearing during the worship service. He cannot afford to purchase the hearing aids that might help him. He knows that the auditorium is equipped with assistive devices located in several of the front rows. But Joe is self-conscious and does not want to sit up front and use the equipment because that will make it obvious to all that he has the hearing impairment. Joe now stays home and listens to the service by tape with the player set at a volume that he can control.

Joe may be responding to any number of issues related to aging and wellness. Some may encounter negative stereotyping as an "old person" as the body begins to show some of the inevitable effects of long life. Age discrimination and negative attitudes about people with any type of disability do exist. This may make it more difficult for older people to admit to experiencing problems of any type. However, each person does need to adapt his or her behavior and image of self as changes occur in the physical body. It may present a challenge for the older adult to recognize changes and to be able to ask for or accept assistance that is needed to maintain function.

Could it be that Joe's stated reason for staying home is a clue to other problems that interfere with his sense of wellness? Several issues should be explored with Joe. Has he had the support needed to adequately grieve the loss of his wife? Is he eating properly now that he lives alone and never did much of the cooking? Now that he is no longer half of a couple, is he still included in the informal, as well as planned events of couples in the congregation? Does he have undiagnosed depression but has not mentioned the symptoms because he attributes them to "just getting old"? Can someone help him find the money for the hearing aids that are not covered by insurance? Such questions illustrate the ways in which consideration of wellness must involve the total person, beyond simply the physical symptoms that may be present on the surface.

*Spiritual*

Typical advice for people desiring to maintain wellness as they age includes the admonition to stay connected with people and with God. Changes in vision or hearing may make this more difficult for the older adult. Consider the case of Elizabeth.

Elizabeth has many friends, regularly reads her Bible, and is part of a Bible study group at her church. However, she is having trouble seeing well enough to enjoy reading that Bible. The large-print version has letters that are large enough to see, but the book is too heavy for her to comfortably hold with her ninety-two-year-old arthritic hands. A friend brought her a New Testament in large print that was of light weight. The sayings of Jesus were in red print, but the red does not provide enough contrast with the cream-colored pages. The thin pages that contribute to the light weight allow shadows from print on the other side to partially obstruct the words. Even her 250-watt light bulb isn't sufficient to compensate for the visual challenges presented by the print. The thought of listening to rather than reading Scripture does not appeal to her. Elizabeth's friend goes on a search for at least some parts of the Bible that contain print that is comfortably readable. Four cities and five Christian bookstores later, only one book has been located. Elizabeth is now able to read at least the Psalms without assistance or adaptive equipment, except for the higher wattage light bulb. Her friend is still searching for additional books of the Bible so that Elizabeth can remain involved in the Bible study group.

### The church's role

To stay connected with others and with God requires vision, hearing, and communication—both spoken and written. Communication is important for interactions with others but can be problematic for older adults at times. Within multigenerational groups, special thought and attention may be needed so that even the older adults can participate. Several suggestions follow.

Print materials produced by congregations can be made older adult–friendly with just a little attention to the realities of how the aging eye works. Now that computer word processing is in common use, why not run a second set of Sunday worship materials that are formatted to be age friendly? The font or type size should be large, the font clean cut rather than fancy, and the print should be dark on white paper. (Save those neon colored pages for the children and young adults.) These items could include the order of worship, bulletin, and newsletter, and be made readily available to be used by people who strain to read standard print.

Communication with those who are having difficulty hearing can be improved by using several simple techniques. Face the person to whom you are speaking, call their name, and get their attention before you start to talk. Position yourself so that your face is in the light. Talk slowly and clearly, not the rapid rate and sometimes mumbled style so often used by teenagers and college kids. Music groups should avoid using excessive volume on electrical instruments. Not only does this make for more comfortable listening, it may help reduce the risks of added hearing loss for people of any age.

Do we inadvertently create risks for others? For example, an evening worship service is planned, perhaps a Maundy Thursday service. The intent is to create a reverent mood, conducive to reflection and quiet worship.

This mood is created in part by having the room dimly lit, using only candles. The seats have been rearranged into small clusters to facilitate a sense of closeness within small groups. However, consider the response of the older adult who enters such a setting. Immediately, the older adult is at such a visual disadvantage that all they can focus on is how to move about the space safely without tripping, falling, or bumping into someone or something.

### When people become too cautious

Sometimes the actions that older people take to protect their physical health inadvertently lead to other problems. Attempts to avoid falls provide an example. Falls are a major risk factor for older adults, with the risk increasing as the person ages. The consequences of a fall can be serious, such as a fracture of the wrist, spine, or hip. Not only does the broken bone present a problem, but the fact that the person experienced a fall may shake their confidence in walking. The person may then become overly concerned about falls, even limiting their walking in the misinformed belief that they are decreasing the risk of additional injuries. Fall prevention includes attention to adequate exercise to maintain joint mobility and muscle strength, removal of throw rugs and other objects that can trip a person, use of adequate light when moving about, review of medications to determine if that might be a contributing factor, and learning to change from a sitting to standing position slowly to allow the body time to adjust to the change.

### Medications

Even people with chronic diseases can experience wellness. Added years of life provide the opportunity for us to encounter more situations and disease conditions that can negatively affect function. Some of these conditions may require medication, and these need to be taken correctly so they promote wellness rather than compromise it. Several terms are important to the discussion of medication used particularly for the older adult. The first is adverse drug reaction, or undesirable response from prescribed medications. The second term is over-the-counter (OTC) medications, or any medication, drug, or pill that can be purchased without a prescription. A third term is dietary supplements, or products marketed as ingredients found in foods, but produced in concentrated forms and high doses.

What exactly is considered to be medication? We cannot rely on the distinction that if the product requires a prescription, then it is a medication. Increasingly, drugs that were once only available by prescription are now being marketed for OTC sales. Additionally, products that are labeled as dietary supplements or "natural" products may have drug-like effects. Labeling of the product as a dietary supplement usually means that the product does not fall under the protective guidelines of governmental regulations.

Older adults are more likely to take medications (prescribed as well as OTC ones) than are younger people for a number of reasons. The risk of undesirable drug reactions increases with the number of drugs being used. Normal age-related changes in the body affect how drugs are absorbed, distributed throughout the body in protein and fat tissue, broken down or handled by the liver and excreted. There can be interactions between different drugs, between prescribed drugs and OTC drugs, herbal products, and even naturally occurring foods. Do not be surprised if the dose of medication prescribed for a seventy-five-year-old is different (usually a lower dose) than for a forty-five-year-old.

So what should the consumer do? Recognize that

items such as herbs, dietary supplements, and OTC products can interact with prescription medications, sometimes in undesirable ways. Develop a healthy skepticism about products advertised on TV and in print media. Just because a product is marketed heavily does not mean that it is really the best one to use. Inform your healthcare provider of all the prescription, as well as nonprescription products, you are using. Carry a list of all prescribed and OTC medications and all herbal or natural products you are using. Show this list to your physician or nurse practitioner when discussing health issues. Read the product information that comes with medications—then ask questions of the pharmacist, physician, or nurse practitioner if you do not understand how the medication should work for you.

The effectiveness and toxic levels of certain medications need to be monitored periodically. Remember to keep your appointments for lab work or a return visit to the healthcare provider. If a prescribed medication does not have the intended effect or if you have an adverse drug reaction, notify the person who prescribed it. They need that information to properly evaluate your condition and perhaps select a different product.

It would take a whole book (perhaps even several) to address all the specific ways in which people can attain personal wellness. With much information on the market and on the Internet, one challenge is to wisely select the resources to read and the guidelines to follow. When in doubt, consult your healthcare provider. Just because something is in print or on the Web does not guarantee that it is useful, safe, wise advice.

Some claim that having adequate money helps a person successfully adjust to the challenges of old age. At times there may be some relatively simple solution to a problem that would allow an older adult to continue to function at their capacity or reduce their risk of injury. However, the solution may involve added cost or may require the hassle of finding someone to reliably perform a service. Examples include the installation of grab bars in the bathroom at the tub and commode to decrease the risk of falls, repair of stairs and railings, or even the purchase of hearing aids or glasses. Although money cannot buy health, happiness, or wellness, adequate money does permit a person to purchase products and services that simplify living.

Scriptures often used when referring to aging imply situations of adversity, trouble, weakness, and despair. Psalm 71:9 says, "Do not cast me off in the time of old age; do not forsake me when my strength is spent." Ecclesiastes 12:1 cautions readers to think about God while they are young, "before the days of trouble come and the years draw near when you will say, 'I have no pleasure in them.'"

Such images do not accurately reflect normal healthy aging in today's Western world, or at least not for those with enough resources to meet their daily needs. It is that link between availability of resources and healthy aging that presents challenges for many older adults today, and can also present opportunities for service within the church family. Perhaps one outcome of discussions about aging can be the discovery of ways to increase the amount of informal helping of one another that takes place within congregations.

# CHAPTER 5

# Redirection: Opportunities Ahead

By Barbara K. Reber

> If people relegate me to the sidelines, I'm gonna
> surprise 'em! Volunteer. Entertain. Get a group
> together and do something.
> —Rhoda Cressman

*H*omer is a retired pastor whose first wife died. LaRue was married to a pastor and her husband died. So Homer and LaRue had many things in common when they got married in 1992. They shared interests in helping people less fortunate than themselves, travel, global missions, and world-wide development and relief efforts like Christian Rural Overseas Program (CROP) and Heifer Project International. Both had already participated and were active in a variety of volunteer and mission projects. For many years LaRue had chaired the annual CROP walk in Charleston, South Carolina, where she lived.

They appear to be having the time of their lives in retirement. For the last several years they have volunteered two months during the summer at Heifer Project International's headquarters in Little Rock, Arkansas. Heifer Project is a development organization that helps people feed and take care of themselves by giving them a cow, sheep, goat, chicken, or other locally appropriate animal that recipients in turn breed and continue the gift of livestock to another needy family.

In Little Rock, it is hot, unglamorous work and maybe it doesn't have the exotic appeal of working in another country, but it is work they believe in deeply. They come back to their church as passionate supporters of Heifer Project and as they share about their experiences, the young children of the church enthusiastically begin collecting pennies, nickels, and dimes to put in little plastic animal arks for Heifer Project. Without intentionally planning to, they have gotten many in their church involved in a meaningful new effort.

They also enjoy occasional trips overseas to keep them in touch with work they enjoyed earlier in places like Haiti and Central America. On a week-to-week basis at home, they help in the Clothes Closet ministry of their local congregation, sorting, hanging, and giving out free clothing to people from Spanish-speaking countries, Russia, Iraq, and the U.S. And these are only a few of the activities that keep them busy and loving this stage of their lives.

Aging is truly an opportunity to either do what you never had the chance to do before or capitalize on the skills and interests acquired over a lifetime and use them in new ways. In this chapter, we will take a look at how to use leisure time in retirement. When we think about aging we are often reminded of the negative aspects facing us. This is necessary, in part, but here we want to look at the possibilities. I hope you will find at least one new idea you might want to pursue in your later years.

It is good to do some serious thinking about where your life is headed during the next twenty or thirty years. What will it be like? I hesitate to use the word *retirement* and search my Bible for references on retirement. I have yet to find any. I like to refer to that part of life's journey as "redirection."

Some people launch second or third careers, either paid or unpaid. You don't have to have lots of money to be able to cut loose in retirement. Not all activities take lots of money. Many times your only expense is the cost of getting there; room and board are then provided.

Eugene Wingert wrote:

The [aging] journey is a series of ups and downs, highs and lows. Sometimes the upward trail is exhilarating and challenging as one exults in the extension to new limits of body, mind, and spirit. The summits reached are enriched in proportion to the effort expended in reaching them. At other times the climb is hard—an uphill battle against a world arrayed against us. Every step is an effort. Struggle is the name of the game. There are peaks of pain. There are peaks of pleasure.

The path downhill is often a relaxed descent into the quiet valley with its cool streams—easy going, a light step, and filled with anticipation of delights to come. The descent can also be a tortured journey into despair, a depressing return to the valley of routine. There is a feeling of emptiness—that only what is left behind has meaning and what lies ahead is vain. There is the valley of delight. There is the valley of despair.

Sometimes the path is level, neither up nor down, easy, unobstructed and smooth. We like it smooth, but the level path is not the place of growth. It is in the highs and the lows, the journey up and the journey down, that we pass our routine comfort zone and open anew to growth.

### *More than doing nothing*

David Mumaw, retiring from thirty-plus years as a noted and beloved high school biology teacher, in an interview described his anticipation for years of hunting and outdoor adventures as follows: "Every night is a Friday night, every morning is a Saturday morning, and there is never a Monday morning."

But moving from a structured lifestyle to one of leisure is a transition that many find challenging. That first month can be all that you hoped for: no schedules, no committee meetings, no reports to write, no hitting the time clock, no brown bag lunches or long lunch meetings, or the interruptions of other staff needing just five minutes of your time. Those who look forward to retirement as a time of only doing nothing are likely to become bored very quickly.

Your time (all twenty-four hours) is yours to do all the things you have always wanted to do: clean the closets, play golf, lunch with friends, put pictures in albums, spend more time with your spouse, friends, or family. And then you turn the calendar and see the blank page. You wonder how you used to do it all.

During more than seventeen years of working in the field of aging, I heard many personal experiences of what this last third of life's journey meant for people. They have time to meditate on life in a new way and many found themselves asking, "Who am I really? Why am I here? What is life really all about?" These questions often echo the questions of the adolescent years and are good questions for discussion. Older adults can be directed in their search for meaning by the belief systems of their faith community. For some older adults this will be from their own congregation, while for others the belief system will go in new directions.

A great deal of ambiguity permeates our thinking

about aging. Is it a decline or an ascent? Should we describe life as a journey that moves upward until it peaks at middle age and then slopes downward to death? Shall we work to prevent aging or learn to revere it? We cannot learn to understand aging if we undervalue or overvalue its realities, or if we simply try to make it appear as much like midlife or youth as possible.

Most retirees leave the workplace while healthy and still active, giving them the opportunity to fill their time with travel and recreational activities. How many times have we seen the bumper sticker, "I am spending my children's inheritance"? However, many give generously of their time to volunteer opportunities that benefit the younger generations or their peers. It would be wrong to recognize only those who spend all of their time playing golf, shuffleboard, or on cruise ships. Many enjoy a combination of leisure and activity after they retire from full-time careers. Some continue to work in part-time jobs to supplement fixed incomes. Others just find work fulfilling. Many provide role models for younger workers.

The fact is that aging is both descent and ascent, both loss and gain. This is also true about every stage of the life-cycle. *Time* is both life and death. Change encompasses both emerging and perishing. At every point in the human journey we find that we have to let go in order to move forward in the journey. Letting go means dying a little. It's a little like what Jesus said: "For whoever wants to save his life will lose it, but whoever loses his life for me will find it" (Matthew 16:25).

### Spirituality

A spirituality of aging should help us find a way to turn losses into gains, to learn how the stripping process which sometimes accompanies aging can be a gradual entrance into freedom and new life—how it can be winter grace.

Winter is a season of some real losses: flowers are gone, leaves fall, trees stand bare, but winter reveals that which summer conceals. We can see further and with clearer vision. We can walk in places that had been filled with brush and leaves, which allows for a new inner life to awaken. Beneath the shell of the bud is sap in gestation. Someone has said, "I bloom indoors in the winter like a forced forsythia; I come in to come out." When we think of spirituality and aging we must define what is meant by spirituality. It is not one compartment of life, but the deepest dimension of all of life.

The spiritual is the ultimate basis for all our questions, hopes, fears, and loves, our efforts to deal creatively with retirement and to find a purpose in this journey after our family has been raised or we struggle with the loss of a spouse. Questions of self-worth, fear of reaching out to make new friends, discovering new talents, finding deeper peace, and expanding our boundaries of love—all these are spiritual concerns. Christian spirituality involves the entire human person in all of his or her experiences and relationships.

A spirituality of aging must begin with our very existence as older people. It calls into question the deepest values of our civilization.

### Service opportunities

Our denomination has for many years provided opportunities for young people to serve the church in a variety of ways. My husband, Don, and I treasure the experience we had early in our marriage to serve in the first Summer Service Unit in Saginaw, Michigan, for the Mennonite Church.

But it took some years of effort and experimentation before successful volunteer programs for older adults came into being. Service Opportunities for Older People

(SOOP) is now a widely recognized volunteer program through which older adults can serve, a program I directed for many years. Other denominations and groups offer similar programs as well. People can choose from a variety of locations and are able to designate the amount of time they wish to make available. The first couple to accept this challenge helped start a silk screening project in Phoenix, Arizona, giving needy people training and an opportunity to create something useful.

Another couple I will always remember was introduced to me when a pastor called and said, "Barbara, there is an older couple in our congregation that is considering some kind of service, will you talk to them?" He added that their gifts would be greatly missed in their small congregation, but they would be happy to release them for this new experience. They came, they served, and on their return they were so happy and excited about their involvement they said, "This may surprise you, but we want to do it again." This couple continued to serve each winter for the next five years. They have been an encouragement to many others.

Another pastor took three months of his sabbatical to volunteer doing something different as he also wanted first-hand knowledge of the opportunities older adults in his congregation were experiencing in the SOOP program. He and his wife highly recommend this experience for other church leaders.

The wife of a much-traveled church worker told me, "My husband is going to be gone for ten days. Is there any place I could serve for this short period of time? He always has interesting stories to relate when he returns and I would like to have something special to share with him." How thrilling it was to hear from her and her husband about her contribution to others during this brief time.

There are many opportunities for older adults to use their gifts today. God is at work in the lives of so many people. In Ephesians 4, we are encouraged to believe that each one of us has received gifts from Christ that are to be used in ministry to others.

### Local service

A good way to get lasting meaning out of life is to spend it in service to others.

There are so many opportunities for service, and many of them are available without traveling anywhere. Our newspapers frequently publish long lists of local organizations needing volunteers, such as hospitals, libraries, service organizations, churches, and schools.

For anyone with teaching skills or interest in acquiring them, there is a huge need right now in the area of teaching English as a second language. Schools are also in need of volunteer tutors in many subjects.

You can serve at a Ten Thousand Villages store (selling crafts from around the world with profits going back to the crafters), helping at a senior center, or reading or writing letters for people with poor eyesight. Many organizations beyond the church offer service opportunities. Joining Lions Club or Ruritans or another service club gives you the opportunity to stay in contact with people in the community outside of church. For instance, the Lions specialize in issues related to sight and hearing and organize collection centers for discarded glasses, mobile screening vans offering free hearing tests, and medical mission trips to countries underserved by eye doctors. If you love animals but hate to be tied down with a pet during retirement years, you can volunteer at an animal shelter giving the unwanted pets exercise and playtime.

The list of volunteer opportunities at just one retirement center gives a great idea of the volunteer possibilities that are available in almost every community—surely something for every interest:

Auxiliary:
- Help with monthly birthday parties in Health
  Care and Assisted Living
- Plan and host events at the Senior Center

Healthcare:
- Meal assistant
- Deliver ice water
- Deliver mail
- Wheelchair escort
- Assist with excursions, special activities
- One-on-one reading, writing
- Mending
- Clothing care
- Gift shop clerk

Direct resident services:
- Deliver Meals on Wheels
- Clean coolers used for Meals on Wheels
- Transportation to medical appointments
- Take items to recycling

Religious life:
- Song leader or accompaniment
- Lead Bible study
- Coordinate services

Senior center (activity center):
- Host/hostess, usher
- Operate popcorn machine
- Water plants
- Maintain bulletin board
- Operate VCR, video camera
- Sing with singing group
- Library assistant
- Computer instructor
- Musical entertainment
- Engrave nametags/signs

### Service in other countries

Every denomination and scores of nonprofit organizations look for volunteers who can serve at locations around the world. Check with your denominational mission office to get information on possibilities. A well-known program is China Educational Exchange, where you teach English at various university settings in China. Habitat for Humanity needs volunteers to build houses both in the U.S. and at their overseas locations. There are usually openings for office and professional work as well as the more physical, manual work.

### Disaster service or other temporary work

Some people feel a special call to respond when disasters happen. They purposely keep their schedule flexible knowing that when disaster strikes, they can drop everything and travel quickly to where they are needed. This is an area where younger people often simply do not have the same kind of freedom. Mennonite Disaster Service and Emergency Response/Service Ministries (formerly Brethren Disaster Service) are two of the Anabaptist-related emergency response organizations that accept volunteers of any faith, and many denominations have similar organized disaster response work.

### Travel

Many people approach the retirement years hoping that they will have the time, money, and good health to travel. If a spouse dies, we may think that we would no longer enjoy travel. Three women, Susan, Doris, and Marian (names changed) are all single. Two of them have been divorced, one never married. None of them are rich but they have discovered they make amicable traveling partners for each other, and for the last several years have traveled to Europe or other locations. This past summer they participated in an

Elderhostel in Wales for three weeks. They stayed in university housing and took the Elderhostel classes, learning about Welch history and culture. A highlight was experiencing a bit of the local culture by joining singing groups as they sang impromptu in local pubs. Elderhostel, of course, offers courses and excursions in many locations in the U.S. as well, and there may even be classes in your area that you could participate in at a very low cost.

### The importance of hobbies

Often when we think of preparing for retirement, we think only of how to save money and what our health will be like. We prepare by exercising and eating properly. But what about preparing in the area of hobbies and what we do with our leisure time?

The busy child-rearing years often allow little or no time for genuinely pursuing our own hobbies. We chauffeur kids to their soccer clubs and dance classes—but what about Mom or Dad? And so as children leave home, it is important to return to hobbies we enjoyed earlier or to find new ones.

Larry always enjoyed blacksmithing, but he had little time to do anything with the various pieces of equipment he collected over the years. When he retired, he helped to organize a blacksmith guild that sets up displays at area fairs and craft shows, giving demonstrations of the ancient art of blacksmithing. He gets to enjoy his hobby while at the same time helping to ensure that future generations also know about this skill.

Richard started an antique bottle collection during his years as a pharmacist, and after he retired he had the opportunity to set up a fascinating, museum-quality display in their basement recreation room. He also attends bottle- or pharmacy-related shows where he has the opportunity to trade, barter, and talk shop with others.

### Specialized professional skills

Maybe helping people who are falling asleep in their wheelchairs participate in sing-alongs is not your idea of what you want to do in your later years. Doctors, nurses, and others in the medical professions will find their skills in much demand as volunteers locally—at free clinics, retirement centers, and health centers—as well as around the world. Bookkeepers, accountants, CPAs, and financial consultants are also much needed. In addition to supplying actual services, you can mentor aspiring young people in your field.

There are many other ways to walk the journey before you. You may wish to continue your education, finish a degree that was interrupted earlier in life, or simply audit some courses in which you have an interest or to learn a new skill that you did not have time to pursue earlier. Intergenerational learning in a classroom is a wonderful experience. Have you thought about writing your own story for those who follow?

In planning your continuing journey, do not forget to nurture self, care for your health, and your spiritual well-being, for in so doing your life can be a great blessing to others. One denomination holds a sporting event especially for seniors. Seniors come together and compete against each other in modified Olympic-style events. The purpose is to encourage participants and the church to embrace a responsible, holistic philosophy of life that includes spirit, mind, *and* body.

People spend a third of their lives learning, a third working, and a third of their lives doing: _____. You can fill in the blank as to how you will spend that last third. It is your choice.

Five thousand people in America turned sixty-five today, tomorrow another five thousand will join them. That is 325,000 candles on an anniversary cake. Every person is like a tree with roots, leaves, blossoms, and with fruit that changes with the seasons. This time of your life, like all times, is a very good one if we know what to do with it.

At each significant change of direction in our lives, we like to leave something of value to those who follow. This was shared with my co-workers at my farewell:

*I give you praise, God of my journey,*
*For the power of love, the discovery of friends, the truth of*
  *beauty*
*For the wonder of growth, the kindling of fidelity, the taste*
  *of transformation*
*For the miracle of life, the seed of my soul, the gift of becom-*
  *ing*
*For the taste of little dyings which have strengthened me*
  *for this moment*
*For the mystery of journey, the bends in the road, the pauses*
  *that refresh*
*For the faith that lies deep enough to permeate discourage-*
  *ment and anxiety.*
*I give you thanks, God of my journey,*
*For all I have learned from the life of Jesus of how to say*
  *good-bye*
*For those who have always stood near me and given spir-*
  *itual energy*
*For your strength on which I can lean and your grace by*
  *which I can grow*
*For the desire to continue on, for believing that your power*
  *works through me*
*For being able to love so deeply, so tenderly, so truly*
*For feeling my poorness, my emptiness, my powerlessness*
*For believing that you will care for me in my vulnerability.*
*I ask forgiveness, God of my journey,*
*For holding on too tightly*

*For refusing to be open to new life*
*For fighting off the dying that's essential for growing*
*For insisting that I must be secure and serene*
*For ignoring your voice when you urged me to let go*
*For taking in all the goodness but being reluctant to
     share it*
*For doubting my inner beauty*
*For resisting the truth of my journey home to you.*
**I beg assistance, God of my journey,**
*To accept that all of life is only on loan to me*
*To believe beyond this moment*
*To accept your courage when mine fails*
*To recognize the pilgrim part of my heart*
*To hold all of life in open hands.*

—Author unknown, adapted by Barbara K. Reber

CHAPTER 6

# What the Finances Say: Financial, Legal, and Other Matters

By Suzanne H. Kennedy

> If anyone does not provide for his relatives,
> and especially for his immediate family, he
> has denied the faith and is worse than an
> unbeliever.
> —1 Timothy 5:8

*M*y work in the financial and charitable giving arena brings me into contact with a steady stream of people from middle age to the truly old. They represent the full spectrum of understandings and behaviors about the personal legal and financial realities of our times. Some are, or soon will be, out of resources. Others have enough to provide for themselves and their families and make regular offerings through church and gifts to charity besides. Most are living active and productive lives whether or not they still earn income. All want competent counsel and appreciate a sense of being cared for.

I need both the facts of their lives and a listening ear to construct a picture of their circumstances for planning. As I record words and numbers in black and white, they add the living color of their lives, such as:

–Encouraging testimonies about God's provision and generosity
–Gratitude for parents who taught and modeled good planning and financial restraint
–Hopes and plans for the future
–Regrets over decisions they've made or put off too long
–Concerns that the rules may have changed and they missed the cues

They have questions. Where are they now? Where should they be going? How do they get there? Who can help? Where is the church in all this?

These needs and concerns of aging people are broader and deeper than one person can serve, and intentionally teaming up with other advisors works well. Another financial services professional and I had compiled a written summary for a senior saint and his family after several meetings and poring through stacks of legal documents, financial statements, and notes. As I shared this overview with a local bank's trust officer, he commented, "You all really take care of your old people."

The other advisor and I were gratified, as Christian business people in the Anabaptist tradition, to be perceived as caregivers. We appreciate being discipled in a faith community that has traditionally given the elderly a place of respect and want to meet their needs, even though the nature of their contribution to the community changes in old age. When spiritually motivated people with appropriate expertise provide biblically based guidance in caring relationships, financial pastoral care can become a reality.

### Cultural issues

It's helpful to put aging in the larger cultural context as we consider how to respond individually and as a

church community. Two pervasive contemporary attitudes related to aging with implications for financial and
legal concerns are the glorification of youthfulness and
the expectation of lifelong consumerism.

When physically attractive young adults serve as the
societal standard, maturing brings the inevitable realiza-
tion that in the world's eyes, we no longer measure up.
Getting older has been about getting worse, not better,
and the cosmetic effects of aging are to be dealt with,
minimized, even altered. We're told to take charge of our
lives and take this anti-aging business seriously. Many face
aging with a certain sense of dread and anticipate it as a
time of losses.

The glorification of youthfulness and the cultivation of
a craving for material things come together in a powerful
way in consumer product advertising. The consumerism
that helps drive our economy is taught early and rein-
forced as a desirable lifelong activity. "Use it up, wear it
out, make do" has been replaced by "use it for a while,
toss or replace it, upgrade if possible." The biblical idea
of simple living has given way to simply living it up, and
"shop 'til you drop" is no longer intended as a joke.

### Turning points

The baby boomers, the bulge in the population born
between 1946 and 1964, are maturing and will be an
increasingly powerful political, economic, and societal
force. Their sheer numbers will stretch resources for the
elderly, but they will have the political clout to influence
government policies that affect them, if they choose to
use it. Much is also being said about the transfer of wealth
from the present generation of elderly to those currently
middle aged. Even though that wealth will not be evenly
distributed, the financial resources it represents offer the
potential for good choices as well as bad.

Youthfulness as the standard is already in the early stages of being displaced as the baby boomers mature. Their spending will gravitate to products and services with which they can identify. The marketing of consumer products and services will move accordingly to reflect the changes and challenges of this group as it ages.

We have a long way to go before a jury of our global peers could convict us of living the simple life, but excessive consumption has been enabled by economic prosperity. For those of us who have not lived through an extended period of nation-wide hard times, economic growth and the opportunity to increase personal wealth are the norm. The frugality of previous generations and those who advocate restraint may have received little attention in the immediate past, but economists and people who lived through the Great Depression of the 1930s have something in common: they know hard times can come. We may get a shove in the right direction when an economic downturn forces us to reduce consumer spending and bursts the consumer debt bubble.

### You and your professional advisors

For the maturing Christian, responsible financial stewardship means making good choices guided by biblical principles. Our responsibility is to gain an understanding of what needs to be planned for and the basics involved in carrying out those plans. Financial and legal realities are far more involved than they were just a generation ago, and planning for and carrying out plans for aging isn't a self-taught, do-it-yourself activity. Information overload often introduces unnecessary fears and frustrations—more information is not necessarily better. You need the counsel and assistance of professional advisors.

We of the faith community need wisdom in walking through these times together and discernment in planning, preparing, and accessing resources for ourselves and those we care about. Competent professional advisors who share, or at a minimum respect, faith values need to be an integral part of the process. There are those within the Anabaptist and larger Christian community who understand the workings of the systems in which we must operate in planning for and living through our older years. Many of them work within the systems themselves and are supported through the services and products they provide. It is appropriate to extend the respect traditionally shown to education, social service, and healthcare professionals within the church to the financial, insurance, and legal professionals who serve us in this way.

### Biblical financial principles

It's impossible to address finances from a biblical perspective and avoid the expectation that our lives mirror both God's generosity and provision, and a measure of fiscal restraint. Talking about finances within the church is stifled in part because we enjoy the freedom not to have specific expectations about giving or spending placed on us by the church, especially the one we actually attend. Those who openly endorse frugality and financial faithfulness may be perceived as holdovers from a time when enforced simplicity and restraint left fewer choices to the individual. Tithing as a *voluntary* spiritual discipline seems compatible with freedom in Christ and a healthy practice of self-restraint.

Basic financial principles haven't changed since Jesus' time, and in his teaching he spoke often and eloquently about the same circumstances which concern us today. Some biblically based principles that pertain to aging issues and related financial concerns:

–Take the elderly seriously and honor them as repositories of wisdom and experience, especially if they are your parents (Titus 2:1-5, 1 Peter 5:5, Matthew 15:4, Ephesians 6:2-3).

–Acknowledge that you share in the responsibility for your own family, including your immediate relatives and the larger church family and community (John 19:26-27, 1 Peter 3:1-7, 1 Timothy 5:3-10, Acts 6:1-5, James 1:27).

–Understand that plans for the future should include the possibility that you may not be here to carry on (John 19:25-27, James 4:13-15).

–Estimate the costs of your plans to see if your resources are sufficient to finish what you intend (Luke 14:28-30, Proverbs 19:2).

–Seek advice and counsel from others who share your values and beware of those who don't (Proverbs 15:22, Matthew 16:12, Luke 16:11).

–Be generous, as God is generous, and give as a spiritual act, especially if you're rich. God decides how much is enough based on motive (1 Timothy 6:17-18, Romans 8:32, Luke 21:1-4).

–Give according to ability, make your giving decisions in the right place—your heart—and carry them out freely and cheerfully (1 Corinthians 16:1-2, 2 Corinthians 9:6-11).

–Give yourself completely and continually—you are the "coin of the realm" of the kingdom of God, made in the image of the King and bearing his likeness (Matthew 22:19-21, Genesis 1:27, Romans 12:1, Luke 16:13).

–Don't spend more time on the basics of life than is necessary but focus instead on things of lasting value and contentment (Luke 10:41-42, Luke 12:22-34, Philippians 4:12-13).

### Preparation as the church

Without doubt the church has not strayed as far as the world from the biblical tenet of the inherent worth of all people. Even so, the value our culture places on youthfulness has tinged attitudes toward aging and the aged within the church. We may love our elderly, but we may not be giving them the place of honor and respect called for by the faith values of our community. We turn to the media and our secular peer group for understanding and practical advice more often than the wisdom treasuries within our midst.

A fresh study of the biblical guidelines for attitudes and behavior toward the elderly would seem in order. An appropriate beginning is to diligently search the Scriptures ourselves. We are responsible for our own biblical literacy and need to balance the interpretations of others, however good their credentials may be, with our personal encounters with the living Word.

Likewise, learning what the Bible says about the material world doesn't come without genuine effort on our part. There is plenty of material available about how to handle your money as a Christian, but it can be startling to realize that while it usually agrees in principle, it certainly doesn't agree about practice. Many Christians place a high value on consensus and process, and we need a common biblical base from which to proceed.

### General retirement planning

Lynn Miller, a stewardship minister with Mennonite Mutual Aid (MMA), likes to say stewardship is "the act of organizing your life so God can 'spend' you." What a fresh perspective for retirement planning and one that is totally in tune with the value of giving ourselves. Our experiences and abilities are a valuable financial resource that we may choose how to spend in retirement.

Retirement planning is a natural extension of basic

financial planning, with income, insurance, and investment considerations all part of the mix. When we begin good financial habits and planning early in life, we are already preparing for retirement.

Clearly the goal is to have enough resources to meet our basic needs and enable a quality of life that blesses us and allows us to bless others. MMA/Mennonite Foundation and Brethren Benefit Trust/Brethren Foundation are two church-related organizations offering resources in this area.

The MMA educational publication, *Living for Today to Anticipate Tomorrow: Saving for Retirement Gives You Choices*, lays out the basic questions in retirement income planning and offers important considerations. These include how you want to live, how much income you expect to need (70 to 80 percent of pre-retirement income is a common planning figure), how you have prepared so far, and what else you need to do. Your retirement is your responsibility, and you should expect to consult a financial advisor for assistance with this part of the process.

Retirement is a multi-stage time of life and may encompass up to one third of a person's lifespan due to longer life expectancies. Another MMA educational resource, *Creating the Retirement of Your Dreams: Making a Successful Transition to the Next Stage of Life*, includes a list of questions pertaining to legal and financial planning that you should address and resolve as you proceed. What's right for your neighbor may not fit your situation, so specific advice is beyond the scope of this chapter. It will have to be sufficient to say that you'll need to make decisions about income, debt, housing, insurance, savings, and the legal considerations for medical and financial decisions and distributing assets at the end of your lifetime.

Remember to consider charitable giving in your ongoing financial needs and plans. You have probably been giving throughout your lifetime, and there are creative and tax-wise ways to continue. Non-cash gifts such as real estate, investments, and life insurance offer possibilities, and some gift plans even provide an income during life and before passing the gift on to charity. Giving through your estate can take a variety of forms, too. You may discover that making charity the beneficiary of life insurance or retirement plan assets has better tax consequences than simply naming charity in your will or trust. MMA offers advice and assistance through the Mennonite Foundation for all types of gift plans and gift assets, and Brethren Benefit Trust/Brethren Foundation provides similar services. Check out your denomination for assistance.

### Estate planning

The MMA publication, *Ensuring Your Assets Become a Witness to Your Values: Planning Your Estate,* says that there are five key stewardship issues in making choices about estates: 1) the money, property, investments and other tangibles entrusted to your care, 2) your legal affairs, 3) emergency medical decisions on efforts made to prolong your life, 4) guardianship of minor children, and 5) providing guidance to your heirs in carrying out your wishes. Estate planning is simply the process of working through these choices, not an elaborate undertaking appropriate only for the wealthy.

Your estate plan, regardless of the size of your estate, has three basic elements: your will and two other legal documents empowering someone to act on your behalf when you cannot. A power of attorney for legal and financial matters includes provisions for when it may be used, such as your physical condition, traveling out of the country, and so forth. A medical power of attorney pertains to all kinds of medical treatment decisions beyond end-of-life issues for the terminally ill.

You will need an attorney to guide you through this process and prepare documents appropriate for your state of residence. The attorney can advise you on the appropriate use of trusts in your planning and make sure your plan not only does what you want but also prevents what you don't want. Attorneys know how to ask questions and include provisions for unanticipated circumstances, such as step-grandchildren or the unexpected passing of a younger and supposedly healthier spouse or adult child.

Before you meet with the attorney, prepare a summary of all you own and owe, including retirement plan assets with their beneficiary designations. List any life insurance policies and their beneficiaries. Also bring complete information on the people whose names will appear in your documents and what their relationship is to you.

The MMA estate planning booklet describes five major duties of an executor: 1) administering your estate (being the project manager for settling things up), 2) making certain types of tax decisions, 3) paying any estate debts or expenses, 4) ensuring that all life insurance and retirement plan benefits are received, and 5) filing the necessary tax returns and paying any federal, state, or local taxes. Your executor is expected to consult with others, including professional advisors, for advice and assistance as necessary.

### Beneficial government programs

We can be thankful for government programs that cover some of the expense for senior services. Social Security is a major factor in retirement income planning, and the federal Medicare system pays for basic health services for all those sixty-five and over, not including prescription drug coverage. Seniors supplement what Medicare covers with private medical supplement health insurance if resources permit. The premium is considerably higher if prescription drug coverage is included.

The state-administered Medicaid program provides funds to pay for long-term care services for those without adequate personal resources. The Medicaid safety net was designed and is operated as a public assistance program and has consequences for the eligible person and the long-term care providers. Not all long-term care facilities accept Medicaid patients. Those that do must keep a balance between those who pay for their own care and those on Medicaid in order to be financially viable. If no space is available for a new Medicaid patient, then the patient goes somewhere else for services until space becomes available.

Residents of retirement communities offering different levels of care receive priority for long-term care services. People coming into retirement communities at levels of care not covered by Medicaid need to be able to pay for several years of care when entering. Those who choose to stay in the family home as long as possible may be surprised at the length of time they remain on a waiting list when they want long-term care at a particular facility, especially if they need to come in as a Medicaid patient.

Medicaid payments to institutions leave a significant gap between the cost of care and the reimbursement amount in many states. The Commonwealth of Virginia in particular has a reimbursement rate well below the United States average. We do our church-related senior service providers a disservice when we expect them to bear the cost of caring for Medicaid patients at the expense of their institutional financial health. The Medicaid gap is a family, church, and community issue.

There have been abuses of the Medicaid system through manipulating the transfer of assets, usually to family members, to become eligible for benefits. As a result states use a variety of approaches including "look back" periods of from three to five years to scrutinize financial transactions in the years prior to Medicaid eligibility. States are becoming increasingly vigilant and look to family members for repayment of Medicaid benefits for long-term care. When a married couple is likely to run out of resources because one of them is or needs to be receiving long-term care, then there are reasonable, legal Medicaid planning steps that can be taken to protect assets for the independent spouse.

There are ethical issues as well as legal issues when people who have assets available to pay for long-term care intentionally make themselves eligible for Medicaid. Even if this is accomplished within the letter of the law, it shifts the financial burden to fellow taxpayers.

### Long-term care insurance

The desire to care for those with long-term care needs continues strong within the church, but the means and methods for doing so are an ongoing challenge for individuals, their families, and churches and church-related service providers. As we age we have concern that we not become a burden to our families, financially or otherwise. With fewer adult children per family and more family members in the workforce, the family's human resources for providing care may be quickly stretched thin.

Long-term care insurance offers both financial protection and care alternatives for seniors and their families, but it has been an area of confusion and misunderstanding. Contrary to the "nursing home insurance" description, this type of insurance may be structured to provide needed services in the home as well as coverage for residential long-term care. The major product decisions pertain to a daily payment amount for service, provisions for that amount to increase as time passes, the number of days you pay before the insurance begins to pay, the number of years or days it will cover, and coverage for home health services.

The perception that long-term care insurance is prohibitively expensive came about because people did not consider it until they were older. Premiums are based on age at purchase, and this is a protection that should be investigated by pre-seniors, as soon as the early fifties. Premiums increase significantly with age at purchase, and a health problem or condition may emerge that puts you in a higher premium category or disqualifies you for coverage altogether.

### The final chapter

Think of planning your own funeral as one more act of caring for those you love. The passing of a family member, especially if it's unexpected, can put a family under time pressure to make financial decisions. An article entitled "Paying for the Funeral" in the May 1997 issue of *Kiplinger's Personal Finance* gave a list of eighteen separate cost items families need to decide besides making choices about the service itself.

Funeral homes encourage preplanning and provide helpful resources. Knowing the expected cost of your funeral lets you plan how to cover those expenses. You may have or put life insurance in place to provide funds, for example. Some consider the prepaid funeral plans marketed through funeral homes. These are financial products (such as life insurance or an annuity) purchased by you that provide an amount to the funeral home at your death toward the expense of your funeral. Be sure you understand which, if any, of the plan benefits are guaranteed, exactly what type of financial product you are purchasing and its risks, and the financial strength and reputation of the company offering the product. It is good practice to have your financial advisor review the plan before purchase.

# CHAPTER 7

# Home Sweet Home: Housing Options

By Pearl Lantz

> Listen to your father who begot you, and do not
> despise your mother when she is old.
> —Proverbs 23:22

## Part I: What Does the Heart Say?

### Images of home sweet home

Recently while I was browsing through a gift shop, my attention was caught by a porcelain, cream-colored meat platter with a border of delicate, Victorian-era flowers encircling the words "Home Sweet Home." Examining it closer, I smiled at the appropriately labeled dinnerware—Nostalgic Houseware.

My mind wandered to similar "home sweet home" plaques that I had seen through the years. What nostalgic images and memories are associated with this simple phrase, and how they differ for each of us!

A plaque that hung in stark contrast to nostalgic memories was this motto in the apartment of a woman at an assisted living facility: "So this isn't home sweet home. Adjust!"

### What makes home sweet?

An elderly friend's home-sweet-home memories centered on the house he had built and the time spent raising his family during some of his most productive years of employment, service, and good health. In later years, he struggled with adjustments of aging and illness and the subsequent move to a retirement community—to the place he disdainfully dubbed "THE Home." He vehemently denounced their tagline, "Making Senior Years the Best Years," and declared that those senior years were not his best years, and the retirement community could not make them the best.

In considering the vast array of housing options open to those preparing for older years, the question, "What makes a living space home?" is a key one. Maybe home sweet home is more a state of being than a place. I recall a sign on a friend's office wall, "I take myself wherever I go." If we are at peace with ourselves, with our neighbors, and with God, maybe our living circumstances are of less importance than we generally think.

Viktor Frankl is an example of one who found deep meaning in life despite horrific circumstances encountered during his imprisonment in concentration camps. For Frankl, the inner decision to find meaning in the midst of suffering ultimately became profoundly more important than the outward horrors he experienced in the camps.

Few of us will ever encounter the horrors Frankl encountered. Yet, most of us will likely experience living situations that fall short of our ideal home. Ultimately, we are left with choices related to our attitudes and decisions related to the how, when, and where of preparing (or helping others prepare) for the older years.

We can approach this latter stage of life with positive action and planning or we can passively wait for others "to take us captive" and make decisions for us. We can anticipate this time with a sense of adventure, and see it as an opportunity to rid ourselves of unnecessary baggage—as a time to prepare for that final journey to our heavenly home—or we can lament "by the rivers of Babylon" as the Israelites did in their yearning for their "home sweet home" of former times.

### In captivity

Psalm 137 vividly portrays the grief of Jewish captives in Babylon after the fall of Judah in 587 B.C.: "By the rivers of Babylon we sat and wept when we remembered Zion. There on the poplars we hung our harps, for there our captors asked us for songs, our tormentors demanded songs of joy; they said, 'Sing us one of the songs of Zion!' How can we sing the songs of the Lord while in a foreign land? If I forget you, O Jerusalem, may my right hand forget its skill. May my tongue cling to the roof of my mouth if I do not remember you, if I do not consider Jerusalem my highest joy" (Psalms 137:1-6).

Their beloved capital, Jerusalem, is in ruins, and only their memories of "home sweet home" provide solace. The scene takes place along man-made canals between the Tigris and Euphrates rivers, where the exiles gather under the trees, possibly after a long, hot day of forced labor. Their bitter memories and mourning for "home" are interrupted by Babylonian captors who taunt them by demanding "songs of joy" rather than lamentation. Not only did the Israelites suffer the indignities of captivity, but they were unable to grieve their loss in privacy.

For many older adults, being forced into housing changes may bring similar feelings of grief and captivity as those faced by the Israelites. Frequently this brings loss of privacy as well. The losses must be acknowledged and lamented before one can successfully move on and achieve integrity (rather than despair) in this stage of life.

### More than conquerors

Again we find inspiration in Scripture: "Who shall separate us from the love of Christ? Shall trouble or hardship or persecution or famine or nakedness or danger or sword? No, in all these things we are more than conquerors through Him who loved us. For I am convinced that neither death nor life, neither the present nor the future, nor any powers, neither height nor depth, nor anything else in all creation, will be able to separate us from the love of God that is in Christ Jesus our Lord" (Romans 8:35, 37-39).

Paul writes to the Roman church prior to his visit as a means of introducing himself, and systematically outlines his understandings of the Christian faith. Rome, as capital of the powerful Roman empire, is experiencing a period of great prosperity, intellectual advancement, and moral decline. The Roman Christians are established and strong in their faith, but will soon experience widespread persecution.

In these verses, Paul reassures the church that nothing can separate them from the ever-present love of God. In the midst of hardships, persecutions, and even death, the Christian finds comfort and victory over adversity and death. A deep faith and trust in God takes precedence over the anxiety and grief generated by adversity, and allows the Christian to experience serenity and a sense of being at home in all circumstances.

Even by the "rivers of Babylon" God's comforting love is present and offers security. Far from being victims of circumstances, older adults and their families can experience meaning and victory in the midst of difficult choices and challenges.

### Our final home

In John 14 we find comfort: "Do not let your hearts be troubled. Trust in God, trust also in me. In my Father's house are many rooms; if it were not so, I would have told you. I am going there to prepare a place for you. And if I go and prepare a place for you, I will come back and take you to be with me that you also may be where I am. You know the way to the place where I am going" (John 14:1-4).

In this Scripture, Jesus is meeting with his disciples at the Last Supper. A sense of uncertainty and fear pervades the room as Jesus tells the disciples of his pending crucifixion, death, and resurrection. Jesus identifies Judas as his betrayer and Peter as one who will deny him. The disciples' secure relationship with each other and with Jesus, as well as their faith, are threatened and shaken. Yet, in the midst of this emotional and spiritual turmoil, Jesus encourages them not to be troubled, promises to return again, and reassures them of his ultimate care in their final "home sweet home" in heaven.

Frequently I have heard people jokingly remark that "aging is better than its alternative," meaning, of course, death, and have wondered about that statement. Do we as Christians really believe that life on earth is preferable to the heavenly home Jesus promises for his followers? Rather than avoiding or dreading death, can we learn to see it as the ultimate adventure and most joyous of all graduations?

As Christians and older adults prepare for that final home, a certain letting go occurs, allowing the relocations and downsizing to become an adventure, rather than a grievous task. Serious travelers invariably travel best when traveling light, unencumbered by too much baggage, and our trip toward that heavenly home is no exception.

### Traveling light

Is it possible to travel light in an American culture that promotes consumerism, self-gratification, and the myriad housing options possible only in an affluent society? Do empty nesters need the many things and larger houses of child-raising years, or could these be made available to younger families?

The task of downsizing is a formidable one, involving both physical and emotional stresses. The physical stress is particularly acute for those of us who may be packrats—just the sheer enormity of going through years of accumulated stuff can be overwhelming. The process can also be emotionally draining as it forces us to bid farewell to the previous stage of life and accept the inevitability of the next stage.

Currently, my husband and I are knee-deep in downsizing, and have experienced both the physical and emotional challenges of this work. However, the act of sorting and discarding has also been therapeutic as we have taken the time to relish, reminisce, and relinquish items no longer relevant or necessary.

Letting go and downsizing is different for each of us, but some form of it is important in preparing for older years. Waiting until a crisis hits before beginning to plan always puts us and our families at a disadvantage and may result in forced "captivity" if others make decisions for us.

### Planning pays

Planning and foresight decrease our chances of being taken captive and enhance options, yet there are no perfect solutions. Values and wishes frequently clash with available options, and despite the best-laid plans, circumstances have a way of changing; decisions may need to be remade or altered. However, taking the initiative and starting early—before crises occur—enables more desirable options than when forced choices occur.

A friend tells of his parents' decision to move into a retirement community at the relatively early age of sixty. Some of their peers questioned the premature move, but the couple, after prayer and careful consideration, persisted with their plans. Six years later, the husband died very suddenly and unexpectedly, and his grieving widow was spared the additional upheaval of selling the family farm and relocating. Not only was she already settled, with new friendships among neighbors, but they had enjoyed the opportunity of creating shared memories in their new home prior to his death.

### Getting started

How do we begin planning for future housing needs? As Christians, we have the unique gift of God's presence and wisdom in decision making. As we seek God's leading, rest in his care, and follow his guidance our energy and creativity are released for the planning process.

Taking inventory of resources, circumstances, health, and values is a useful exercise in considering various housing options. A key decision relates to where you will live—in your current community or in a new community? Is it important to live close to family or certain friends, and if so whom? If a move is needed to achieve this, are you (or they) willing to move?

Other questions to consider include:

–Spouse's views and wishes—do they coincide or clash with your own?

–Spouse's health needs and life expectancy— who will likely live longer?

–Proximity of services: hospitals, physicians, wellness centers, home health agencies, transportation, long-term care facilities, and shopping?

–Which is more important—lots of activity and socialization, or privacy and solitude?

–Adequate service opportunities and church connections?

–Status of finances—how much is needed?
–Amount of space needed or desired?
–Desirability of neighborhood, noise level, and crime rate?
–Preference for being with peers or with people of varied ages?
–Importance of pets, personal furnishings, and other personal items, and do options facilitate these?

What other things are important considerations for you? They will vary from person to person, but taking an inventory of essential needs, values, and preferences prior to decision making may help avoid backtracking later.

## Part II: What are the options?

I will list various options for housing, basically in order of least expensive to most expensive, and in order of maintaining most independence to least independence. Some folks approaching retirement decide to sell their home completely and go mobile, buying a home on wheels such as a recreational vehicle or motor home. They travel most months out of the year, visiting children, maybe parking it for the winter somewhere in the south. While this may at first seem like an unstable, transient lifestyle that leads to isolation from community, people who do this find their own meaningful communities among others doing the same thing. Some find it an especially attractive "vehicle" for traveling to and working and living at various service or disaster sites.

And while this sounds like high adventure and an inviting option for some, it can have drawbacks, such as for the couple who sold out, purchased a motor home, and soon after the husband suffered a stroke. Most of us opt for more traditional housing in our retirement years.

### Staying put

The majority of older adults prefer staying in their homes rather than moving, but many homes require adaptations to adequately address the needs of the older years. Some basic considerations include the feasibility of an outside ramp in place of stairs, widened hallways and doors (at least thirty-two inches), and a first-floor bedroom and bath (preferably with turning radius of five feet and a walk-in shower). Other adaptations could include lowered light switches, lowered or adjustable shelving and countertops, grab bars, faucets with levers in place of knobs, telephone jacks in bathrooms and frequently-used rooms, handrails on both sides of stairs, windows and doors that open easily (using levers and cranks), and the addition of an apartment for potential caregivers.

Some older adults may find themselves property rich and cash poor, and require financial help prior to making home conversions. For seniors in this situation, reverse mortgages may be helpful—a type of loan that allows homeowners to convert home equity into a lump sum payment, monthly income, or line of credit. As cash advances are made and interest is added to the loan balance, the debt increases and home equity decreases. No repayments are required until the homeowner sells the house, moves away, or the last surviving borrower dies. Reverse mortgages are helpful, but can be complicated, and consultation with financial advisors and attorneys is advisable.

In-home services are also an important component for people choosing to remain in their homes. A large and diverse network of providers offers in-home assistance with such tasks as housekeeping, laundry, meals, transportation, shopping, errands, medical care, and personal care. Services, agencies, and fees vary with different states and provinces, but referrals and services are frequently found through hospitals, home health agencies, departments of social services, area agencies on aging, and individual providers. If certain medical or financial criteria are met, sources such as Medicare, Medicaid, long-term care insurance, social services, and area agencies on aging may be able to help with costs.

### Homesharing

Various types of creative homesharing options are open to older adults and their families. Shared housing may involve arrangements with non-family members or family members, age cohort or intergenerational groups, and be elder initiated, agency assisted, or agency sponsored. The term "shared housing" generally refers to the practice of two or more people sharing a home where each has private sleeping quarters, but the rest of the house is shared.

Although accessory apartments are a bit different, as they tend to be self-contained, they are a type of homesharing. A widow had her second floor converted into an apartment and then found a young couple who helped with meals, housekeeping, medications, and limited personal care in exchange for rent and utilities. The arrangement proved highly satisfactory for all: the widow received the needed assistance, her family had greater peace of mind knowing that help was available, the young mother was able to achieve her goal of being a stay-at-home mom, and everyone enjoyed intergenerational relationships.

Families may also choose to homeshare, and these arrangements can take different forms. An existing bedroom can be converted or an in-law apartment added. Separate housing units, sometimes referred to as granny

flats or elder cottage housing opportunity (ECHO) housing, provide more separate space and privacy. The Amish
*Grossdawdy* (grandfather) houses are good examples of
families caring for and assimilating older members into
family life. Support services such as adult daycare, respite
care, and in-home services may help the arrangement
function more smoothly, particularly if the older family
member requires significant caregiving. Also, as with any
homesharing, zoning concerns and regulations vary and
should be addressed.

Another type of homesharing may involve two or more
older adults joining forces as housemates. In some such
arrangements, housemates initiate and manage the relationship; others are agency assisted, where a matching service finds suitable housemates. Agencies may help with ref-
erence checks and screening, do personality profiles, assess
compatibility of housemates, and provide assistance with
formal contracts. At times, agencies may help with finding
housing and even assume responsibility for its maintenance and management, as well as the services offered.

Some advantages of homesharing include financial
support, companionship, security, sharing of household
tasks, assistance in emergencies, and help with personal
and medical needs. The disadvantages might involve personality differences, loss of privacy, household management issues, freedom to have company, and inadequate
space. A good way to explore homesharing is to do a trial
period before making formal commitments. The
National Shared Housing Resource Center can provide
additional information regarding referrals and technical
assistance (see website listings in appendix E).

### Planned communities

Planned communities have and are becoming more
popular in the U.S. and Canada. Again, there is a wide

diversity in the way they function and are managed. Some are intergenerational and some are designed for adults only.

Intergenerational communities emphasize the blending of different age groups and household types—couples, singles, families, young and old—into a single community. These communities are largely self-contained, with a mixture of private housing and common areas for socialization, education, and recreation. Extended families, biological or otherwise, can enjoy privacy and independence, yet also experience the proximity of family and group interactions. Some planned communities intentionally include aspects of communal living, enabling young and old to help with each other's needs. Older folks may help with childcare, tutoring, and mentoring, while younger families assist with heavy work or medical needs.

Other planned communities may serve adults only in an age-segregated atmosphere. Many have extensive recreational facilities, secured premises, and offer minimal maintenance. A more limited number have medical services available. Generally, these communities serve young-old (see chapter 9 for a discussion of this term), educated, and well-to-do seniors who are looking for socialization and recreational opportunities as well as desirable neighborhoods and security.

### Congregate living

Congregate housing generally refers to a multi-unit building of self-contained apartments where some common space and supportive services are available. Other terms frequently used are independent living, retirement housing, supportive housing, and senior apartments. Common space may include a dining room where some meals are provided, social and group meeting space, a beauty/barber shop, and recreational space. Optional housekeeping and twenty-four-hour assistance are frequently available as well. Generally, residents are expected to manage their personal and home care needs, although services may be purchased. Congregate housing may be found in stand-alone facilities or be part of a broader retirement community campus, and a wide variety of payment options exist.

Low-cost rental apartments are available through the Department of Housing and Urban Development and USDA Rural Development for seniors and people with disabilities. Federally assisted congregate housing offers a variety of services similar to other congregate housing settings. Rents are calculated differently depending on the program, but usually do not exceed 30 percent of income. To qualify, people must have low or moderate incomes. (Housing vouchers or certificates for private apartments are also available through housing authorities for low-income people of all ages.)

### Residential care

Residential care facilities are identified by many names, including adult foster care, board and care homes, personal care homes, and assisted living. Facilities can range from small to large, accept private or public reimbursement or some combination of the two, and differ widely in the services they offer. A common denominator of all these options is the bridge of services offered between independent living and nursing care.

Adult foster care is typically provided in single-family homes that serve no more than five people. Generally services such as meals, laundry, transportation, and some minimal personal care may be provided. Ideally, the older adult is incorporated into the life of the family and receives emotional support as well as housing.

Board and care homes, personal care homes, and assisted living facilities are very similar in the services offered, but differ in size and regulation. Many board and care homes tend to be smaller and many are unlicensed, operating with minimal oversight from state agencies, while assisted living facilities tend to be larger, more institutional, licensed, and more highly regulated. Generally meals, laundry, housekeeping, transportation, and some degree of personal and healthcare services are provided. Funding comes from state and local reimbursements (for those with limited funds), some long-term care insurance policies, and private payments.

*Nursing care*

The percentage of older adults living in nursing homes at any given time is relatively small—generally about 5 percent, although the chance of people needing nursing care sometime in their lifetime may be as high as 40 percent. Costs are enormous, and average more than $50,000 per year (see website listings in appendix E).

Nursing homes are becoming more user friendly than in the past, although they are still quite institutional in many respects. Here, the medical model tends to prevail, and residents largely respond to nursing decisions related to their schedule and care. However, many are attempting to become more home-like by incorporating gardens, animals, and visits from children (known as the Eden Alternative) into their programs.

The nursing home industry is highly regulated and struggles with nursing shortages, inadequate public reimbursement, and stringent regulations. Some are identified as "skilled" where short-term rehabilitation is provided through Medicare reimbursement, and others are known as intermediate care facilities where chronically frail elders receive substantial long-term care assistance. Potential reimbursement sources for long-term care are limited to Medicaid (for those who have depleted resources), long-term-care insurance, and private payments.

### Retirement communities

Retirement communities abound throughout the U.S. and generally provide a continuum of housing and care options, from independent living to assisted living to nursing care. Some simply provide a continuum of care, with no lifelong guarantees that space will be available in the next level of care when needed. Others provide a life contract and, in exchange for a substantial down payment, guarantee space and care as needed.

In choosing any of the above options it is important to first of all decide where you want to live and then research the options in that geographical area. It is impossible to thoroughly cover all the intricacies and variances that occur with elder housing and services in this chapter—whole books have been written on each, but hopefully this will get you started. In order to make wise decisions, visit various housing programs, talk to people who live there or have used those services, ask questions about life contracts, what happens when private funds are gone, the monthly and daily charges (including ancillary services and additional charges), and ratios of workers to residents. Essentially, research and find out all you can before making commitments.

### Seize the moment!

The choices are vast and limited only by our imagination. Maybe this maze of choices is in itself confusing and overwhelming. Yet, God promises to lead us, to give wisdom as needed, and will walk with us through the process. Enter this stage just as you would the college age: with curiosity, with anticipation, by doing a self-inventory and researching the options.

We are blessed with a wide variety of housing choices, and we have the freedom to create and dream of new options—possibly some not previously explored! Nothing is stopping us from actively and enthusiastically seizing this opportunity of creating our own unique housing option, except the lack of vision and passive inertia that prevents us from dreaming. Choices are vast and are ours to seize.

# CHAPTER 8

# All in the Family

By Ann Bender

> There's a tsunami of caregiving coming. . . .
> It's genuinely unstoppable and our ankles are
> already wet.
> —Ira Byock

*I* have been involved in either studying aging or working with people older than I for the last twenty-seven years of my life. I officially joined them two years ago on my sixty-fifth birthday. All my life, I was drawn to people who were much older.

I was born to an Amish couple who began their lives together living in what we call a duplex. Grandma and Grandpa lived on one side and since my father was the youngest son, he was the one to live next door, a tradition in this Ohio Amish community.

I remember the door, even the doorknob, that led me to my grandparents' kitchen. I was permitted to go to their kitchen often to finish my meal. I can feel the warmth of my grandfather's arms as I sat on his lap. He smelled of spearmint, those soft pink ones. They were always in his pockets for me. I don't remember much of what he said; it seems he was always listening to me. I am told I often made up tales that he appeared to believe. Once when he fell asleep I colored his bald head with my crayons. He seemed to enjoy it.

When I was four years old we moved twenty-five miles away from my grandparents. On one of my overnight visits my grandfather presented me with a child-size hickory rocker which I still have. On that visit I am told that I reminded them that they had "very good company."

These memories and experiences led me to become a dedicated advocate for older people. After I was married, my own family's journey led me to Mississippi, New Orleans, Oklahoma, and Virginia. Still the early memories of visits to grandparents are vivid. Ironically, since my husband and I lived long distances from family, we were not able to become involved in the care of grandparents. My parents gave them much support and our visits to Ohio often included visiting grandparents. Even the care we provided our own parents was from a distance. I experienced some guilt when I compared my own actions with what I truly believe and promoted about family involvement in caregiving. I served as the executive director of the Area Agency On Aging in the Shenandoah Valley in Virginia from 1982 to September 2001. I worked in several other positions for the agency during the five years prior to 1982.

### One family story

Amish families have been examples of family caregiving that at least from a distance appear to be ideal. Following is one example of the system of care that some Amish communities have developed (names changed).

On numerous occasions we visited my father's only Amish brother. A serious stroke left Uncle Edward to live most of his last ten years in a wheelchair. In spite of the stroke he continued to be able to communicate. He often had tears in his eyes when he spoke. His wife, Ida, suffered from osteoporosis so she was unable to provide all the care he needed.

Edward and Ida lived in a small version of their family farmhouse. Their house was attached to the original farmhouse by a small porch. Their youngest son and his family moved into the "big house" when they took over the family farm.

Like many Amish families, Edward and Ida had a large family, four daughters and six sons. Eight of their ten children also have large families. All but two live within a ten-mile radius of their family home. The day we visited, several grandchildren were there to help. It was as if each one was programmed to know without prompting what to do. Though none were more than eleven or twelve years of age, the slightest suggestion sent them to the kitchen for a drink of water or to help their grandmother prepare food.

On one such visit, the family had taken on the task of making noodles. Large masses of egg noodles were lying on clean paper on the floor upstairs to dry. Children were everywhere helping with each little chore. No one asked if they could be excused to go play. There were no arguments about whose turn it was to help. It was like a movie that had been rehearsed. Once when their grandfather asked for ice cream, it appeared from a gas-powered refrigerator in the big house. The grandchildren were eager to bring it to him.

The walls of Uncle Edward's room were covered with pictures that local Amish children had drawn and colored. The whole community knew about his stroke and the family's involvement with his care. We were told that the only time he had any skin problems that are typical of bed-ridden patients was the time he got pneumonia and spent several days in the hospital. He came home with a bedsore. A neighbor, a self-taught nurse, came to help and with some home remedies his skin soon healed.

Traditionally the Amish do not pay into Social

Security. Any expenses they incur at a time like this are taken care of through the neighborhood Amish church. Local physicians willingly provide care for Amish families. They do not have to submit any complicated Medicare or other insurance forms to receive their compensation. If a physician can speak Pennsylvania Dutch, it is an added benefit.

Within several miles this family model was replicated over and over. Although there are exceptions, in most cases the extended family becomes involved in caring for aging grandparents. Food is shared with those in the *Grossdawdy* (grandfather) house. It appears to be an ideal setting for several generations to care for aging parents. With large families, it isn't difficult to send family members to take their turn with the care, and mothers are usually at home. To maintain the family farm and, more recently, small businesses, all family members are needed. Even for Amish families, times are changing.

### Effects of cultural change

During the early twentieth century, farm life made it easy to incorporate older family members into the farm operation. Traditional ways of farming and stories of faith were passed from one generation to another. When the Social Security system was established in 1935 after the Great Depression, age sixty-five was established as the retirement age in the United States. Few people lived much longer. Thus, Social Security was not a tax burden to the country.

As the country became more industrialized, fathers began to get jobs away from the farm to supplement the family income. Mothers stayed at home, so if a grandparent needed a home, it was still possible. Often mothers, grandparents, and children took care of most of the farm chores.

World War II came and many men left to serve. Among pacifist churches, conscientious objectors also were called and many went to Civilian Public Service camps for service assignments and to work in mental hospitals. Women began to work in jobs outside the home. Public funds were used to develop facilities called "old people's homes." Some were referred to as county homes for the poor. Geriatric wards in mental hospitals frequently were home to people who had no one to identify as family. These people did not need mental health treatment. They just had no place to go. In the early 1960s, church conferences such as the Virginia Mennonite Conference, as with many other regional denominational agencies, decided to develop care for older people who had no family to care for them.

The advent of technology not only provided more jobs, it also improved medical technology. In the early 1900s life expectancy was about forty-six, while today it is in the mid seventies. In fact, the population over eighty-five is the fastest growing group of elderly today, with increasing numbers of centenarians.

According to Census Bureau projections, we can expect to see the numbers of older adults double between now and 2030. Already we have a shortage of healthcare workers. Nursing homes and adult care homes find it difficult to find enough workers. According to a recent AARP publication, 90 percent of today's nursing homes are understaffed. Some larger for-profit owners of nursing homes are either going bankrupt or selling out. Other service providers, such as area agencies on aging, are being asked to take major responsibility for finding places for the residents of these institutions. Pressure is put on families to either bring older relatives into their homes or to help pay for the cost of care.

With increasing healthcare costs, more costly regulations to comply with, and greater expectations from the elderly population, "continuing care communities" (retirement communities offering multi-level care) find it difficult to make ends meet. Many denominations are supporting continuing care communities that find it easier to meet the expectations of people who have retirement funds to pay for the upscale lifestyle they want. While our church-supported continuing care communities usually accept a percentage of people who cannot afford the care, they depend on private funds to supplement public funding. I trust we will continue to provide the same level of care to those with no private money or long-term care insurance. According to the Virginia Department of Medical Assistance, the majority who need care in a nursing home deplete their personal funds within two years. If they live beyond those years, public funds are used to pay for their care.

At a recent forum on "Age Power," Dr. Ken Dychtwald, a national visionary and authority on the implications of the aging of America, raised concern about the twenty-five million baby boomers (those born between 1946 and 1964) who will be retiring by 2025 with inadequate savings for retirement.

Those of us who live near younger family members may have the good fortune of having someone around to assist with personal care or home maintenance. However, many older adults may not have that luxury. Younger families frequently require two wage earners to support the high cost of education. Careers may have taken them hundreds of miles away from their parents. Long distance can complicate providing support and assistance for older relatives. If a parent can no longer drive a car, who will provide transportation for doctor's appointments or grocery shopping? Many rural communities do not have public transportation. A recent community survey in the

Shenandoah Valley identified isolation as a significant issue that is often due to a lack of transportation. Other issues identified were a lack of information about available resources and no one to help them link to the system of services.

### Families cannot always be there

There are a number of reasons families can't always help out:

–Families today have an average of two children
–In most families, if there are two parents, both parents are working
–Families often move away from their parents to accept career opportunities

These three facts alone have changed our ability to provide care. However, many families do make serious sacrifices to support their older family members. According to recent information from the Virginia Department for the Aging, more than 80 percent of the elderly rely on family members, neighbors, and friends for support. The burden on these families is eased if local area agencies on aging are actively involved with families.

Family members who live hundreds of miles away from their parents may travel to them over weekends, keep in touch by telephone or e-mail, or help with bill paying and organizing assistance. Community resources such as Meals on Wheels, care management and in-home services, and personal care and homemaker services, may be arranged from a distance. However, many adults feel that having someone they are not acquainted with come into their home is intrusive. Our family was able to find a friend who came in to do some housecleaning and food preparation for my parents. This required private pay, however.

### How do we honor fathers and mothers in the twenty-first century?

Like many questions we face today, we do not find clear-cut answers in the New Testament. Does "honoring our parents" mean visiting them once a year during the family vacation? Does it mean calling them once a week? Does it mean giving up a career and moving back to the family home? It is not uncommon for children to give up a career to move in with a parent to care for them. Is this what the Bible requires of us?

### Can we find a theme in the New Testament?

If we examine the life of Jesus we find a theme of "caring for people." He had a reputation for going "around doing good" (Acts 10:38). Jesus always cared for the vulnerable, blind, poor, or those disliked by society for any reason. He was most critical of the religious community when they questioned his association with sinners and people that didn't stick to the leaders' rules. But Jesus did not forget about his own mother. While he was dying, Jesus asked his disciple, John, to take care of his mother (John 19:25-27). He knew he would not be there to care for her. We are also advised to take responsibility for providing for family members (1 Timothy 5:1-8). How do we translate that into today's world?

Who should take care of our mother or father when we can no longer care for them? We may have as many as five or even six generations living at one time, with the possibility of a seventy-five-year-old caring for a ninety-five-year-old. There are examples of spouses who provide care for each other to the point of exhaustion. The caregiver may develop health problems because they focus on caring for others and not for themselves.

A friend of mine who had a full-time job spent many evenings helping her mother with household chores. She took time off work to take her to doctor's appointments. She often spent evenings helping an uncle with household chores, lawn care, bill paying, and other support services. Her daughter and son live in the community also. She seldom had time to spend with them and her grandchildren because she was so involved with elderly family members. It was not uncommon for her to become ill and spend several days in bed until she could resume her duties again.

### *Role reversal—whose choice is it?*

There are times when dementia and other health problems make it important for family members or some trusted friend or professional to be empowered to make choices for people (power of attorney, discussed in chapters 6 and 10).

We make great efforts at teaching our children to become independent and to make good decisions. At no age do we willingly like to give up the privilege of making our own decisions or being in control of our lives. On the other side, the language we use—even body language—may imply we no longer look to our elderly parents as capable of being in charge of their own lives. Sometimes it seems that gray hair and physical signs of age somehow give those taking care of elderly people the license to use childlike language in addressing them. No matter what our relationship is to an older adult, we must be aware of the importance of their dignity, self-respect, and need for a purpose in life.

# CHAPTER 9

# It Takes a Congregation: Grace Given, Grace Received

By Ken Hawkley

> O God, from my youth you have taught me, and
> I still proclaim your wondrous deeds. So even to
> old age and gray hairs, O God, do not forsake
> me, until I proclaim your might to all the genera-
> tions to come.
> —Psalm 71:17-18

*H*elen (all names changed) was not having a good time. The congregation she and her husband had served in and loved for all these years felt foreign and empty since her husband, George, died. For many years she and George had been what people call "deep-pocket givers." They had always been among the first to welcome newcomers and invite them out for lunch. They had served on committees, participated in Bible studies, and helped to guide the congregation through turmoil and joy. They enabled lay people and pastors alike and supported the many pastors that had passed through in the years since they had joined.

With George suddenly gone, Helen felt like less than half of what she once was. She stopped attending church regularly and was thinking of attending another larger church with a group for widows. Then, a group of people from her own congregation began to phone each other. They had all been touched deeply by Helen and George and wanted to do something. The congregation, which had not had a death for many years, did not have structures or committees set up to minister to those who grieved. Without central leadership or prompting from the church, these concerned people knit a loose web of support around Helen. They would visit her, take her to lunch, go on walks, invite her over for meals, phone her, and send her cards. They were committed to being with Helen throughout her grieving process and beyond. Helen was wrapped in a ministry born of love and caring. As the people supported her, friendships strengthened and she once again felt the vitality of the congregation she had served in.

This story highlights how older adults, who have been a vital part of a congregation, may find themselves on the fringe through various circumstances. None of the caregivers in this story were professional counselors. They simply cared for Helen enough to reach out and bring her back into the arms of the congregation—and into the arms of God. In this way, Helen was able to come back and offer her considerable skills and gifts as she recovered and worked through her grief in a loving, caring environment. Part of the willingness to reach out to Helen was because of the love and grace she and George had showered on the congregation. This made her withdrawal noticeable and the response to extend grace to her more natural.

### Description of the issues

Proper labels are important. For some, the term "elderly" carries the baggage of being frail, slow, physically impaired, and other negative images associated with growing old. I will simply use the term "older adult." Katie

Funk Wiebe, author of several books on aging, subdivides this category into "young old, middle old, and old old." I will sometimes use these descriptions, though I have not defined them further in any meaningful way.

Much work was done in the last half of the last century on human development. It is not helpful to rely too much on theoretical work such as that of Erik Erikson and his stages of psycho-social development or James Fowler and his stages of faith development. While theories like these may be tied loosely to age, we cannot assume that older adults have journeyed along some theoretical developmental path according to a schedule determined by someone else.

Nevertheless, knowing something of these theories of development is helpful for spotting where people, including older adults, are situated in their journey through life. The theories also help us to narrow the field of possible needs and goals of these people in their particular stage of life. Therefore, while it is good to know the research done on human development, we should hold it lightly. Each person will be who he or she is, not who some researcher says they are. We must always remember that research deals in statistics and phenomena; ministry deals with individuals.

In these times, being older does not mean being frailer, slower, or more forgetful. But, as anyone who is older will tell you, older does not always mean wiser. In fact, ministry with older adults is just like ministry with other age groups in the congregation. You have to get to know the individuals before you can know how God wants to use them and what their needs are.

The predominant nature of getting older is an increasing awareness of loss, discussed in chapter 2. One of the current pressing issues for church leaders is to develop a satisfactory theology of loss and suffering. One of the more harmful teachings for some older adults was the idea that those who are faithful are rewarded and receive blessings, while those who are unfaithful receive punishments, hardship, and curses. Guilt arises when health begins to fail and loved ones die and there is a growing sense of isolation and marginalization. All of these things feel like punishment, hardship, and curses, even though the adult may have done all they felt they could to live a Christ-like and faithful life. The conclusion for some is that some past sins have come back and they are being judged. It is the only solution that makes sense to them. How can the congregation work to convince them of their place as loved and accepted members of God's family?

Older adults often come to a stage where they are concerned with passing on some of what they know and have learned to younger generations. They want to pass on things that are important to them in the hopes that those younger will avoid some of the pitfalls they encountered. Older adults also hope to make sure the central beliefs, traditions, stories, and discoveries of the past are not forgotten. In psychology this attitude is called generativity. In our communities of faith it may be called "passing on the faith."

Older adults seem to take two broadly defined paths. There are those older adults who wish to preserve the traditions, beliefs, theology, worship styles, doctrine, and all other aspects of congregational life familiar to them. There are others who are willing and open to change in any or all categories.

It is assumed that all older adults resist change, but that is not true. Some older adults feel that doctrine and worship styles should remain the same, while others are open to questioning and changing these things to better suit a changing society. Some older adults feel that change means that old ways are cast aside without appreciation, that the congregation is on a slippery slope doctrinally, theologically, and spiritually. Some older adults feel that, while change for change's sake is not good, the congregation needs to adapt to new realities that were not present when they were young.

Older adults will deal with change the way they have done so all their lives. In fact, researchers have theorized that generations, called age cohorts, have general characteristics that define that generation throughout the life of its members. Baby boomers, for instance, display a certain innovation for change that is stronger than those generations younger or older than they are. Because of this, sociologists may assume that baby boom older adults will also, as a whole, be more innovative and accepting of change.

Regardless of generational characteristics, however, some older adults gain a more universal perspective. They may see the good in many things and be less judgmental of new things. Some older adults may be able, for example, to hold a strong Christian faith while seeing the truths in other religions. On the other hand, some older adults hold tighter to the beliefs and doctrines they grew up with. They see the gaps between what they believe and what other religions believe. They are more sensitive to the uncertainty of syncretism. In other words, some older adults develop a greater capacity for ambiguity than others.

Whether young old or old old, older adults generally find that relationships grow more important as the years go by. They cherish long-term, trusted friendships and are often eager to meet new friends of their own age and across the generations. As a person advances in age, however, building new relationships may seem to require more and more effort. The older adults get, the less inclined they are to want to expand their fellowship circle if the emotional, psychological, and social effort is more than they feel they have to give.

How can the congregation provide needed care in the years when elders experience long distance family ties and health failures? How can the congregation open doors of opportunity for older adults to serve and be served, love and be loved, give and receive? How can we overcome the stereotypes of what it means to be elderly and live in ministry with those in our midst who are advanced in their years?

In John 21:15-19, Jesus calls his close companion, Peter, to feed the flock of followers that will grow from what was begun during his ministry. It is the juxtaposition of the call to care with the allusion to old age that is intriguing for our study of ministry with older adults. This text summarizes some of what older adults have done and what they fear. Getting old can mean losing power, authority, and a chance to have a say in what happens around you and to you.

Jesus' words may echo the golden rule: "Peter, take this charge seriously and you will reap the benefits of your own care and concern for my sheep when you are older." Like Peter, older adults may hope that the good they have done on behalf of the congregation, their faithfulness, their sacrifices and contributions will mean that generations that follow will continue their work. Older adults realize that they will not always be the guiding forces they once were in congregational life, but they hope that some of what they worked for will last through changes, growth, and new ideas.

In this passage and in the continuing saga of Peter's life we may find the beginnings both of a theology for older adults and a way to minister with them. Peter was obviously favored by Jesus. Peter was one of Jesus' closest companions and friends. The exchange in John 21 between Christ and Peter took place after Peter's denial. Clearly that incident mattered little to the risen Christ at this point. We know from Acts that Peter tried to lead an exemplary life as leader and spokesman for the new group growing in Jerusalem. We also know that he made some mistakes along the way. In other words, Peter was completely human. As we look back over Peter's career, we see that he tried his best to obey Christ's command to "feed my sheep." So we assume that Peter surely received blessings in heaven and was always in God's favor.

In the same way, many older adults have heard Jesus' call to be good disciples. As Jesus demonstrated, short-comings in behavior, even betrayal, are less important than maintaining and deepening the relationship we have with Christ.

We do not receive blessings as a reward for good work. Blessings come as a natural consequence of the good work we do. Good work and good attitude go hand in hand. A good attitude expects good results. Therefore, the person who has a deeper relationship with Christ anticipates blessings. Therefore, the blessings that come from doing good are more apparent.

Perhaps one of the reasons that some older adults have difficulty with loss is that they tend to dwell on why these things are happening. It is certainly appropriate to mourn losses. However, when these losses take control of our lives, we can be steered off course, focusing on the reasons for these "bad things" and assigning them as punishments we deserved. It is then that the faith community can help one another to remember that God loves and accepts us and does not want harm to come to God's special creations. Whether we feel we have done all we could have to be faithful during our life, God loves, accepts, and desires a continued relationship with us.

It is the wish of most older adults to take care of the

sheep in whatever flocks they are a part of. As grandparents, as elders in the congregation, as experienced volunteers, and in so many capacities, older adults want to pass on what they know and want to give gifts of friendship, love, acceptance, and material things to those they appreciate.

### Congregations provide opportunities

An active life is a happy life. Research has shown that people who engage in a variety of activities which are physically and mentally challenging, have better attitudes, have more mental and physical capacities, and age better.

In her book, *The Fountain of Age*, Betty Friedan says that older women who "had returned to or started careers after their children entered school, or who combined homemaking and work, had higher life satisfaction as they aged. The lowest satisfaction was evident among women in a single continuous role—either homemaker or worker—throughout their adult life." Similar studies indicated the same results for older men.

Therefore, older adults who have opportunity for a wide variety of activities will fare better in life generally. The congregation can help by opening up new opportunities for older adults.

Participation in congregational life is best when the diet is a balanced one, with time for prayer and confession, time for study and response, time for singing and joy, time for serving and being served, and time for passing on the faith to others. Older adults do well when they are challenged to do and to be more than they are. That is, they must continue to grow spiritually, intellectually, emotionally, and in other ways. They should use current skills and learn new ones. To provide all this, it takes a congregation.

In order to better organize ministry opportunities, let

us look at the life of the congregation through a four-fold lens as illustrated in appendix A. The four quadrants of that drawing help categorize the arenas of congregational life. Though each quadrant flows into the others in real life, this more static version may help us to see where older adults have plugged into congregational life and where there are still new opportunities. This model is taken from a ministry model developed by Abe Bergen, Eleanor Snyder, and Ken Hawkley. It is called "Opening Doors: Nurturing Faith in the Home and Congregation." It represents a way to think holistically about how we nurture one another.

**1. Worship.** Those who are engaged in the functions of the church may be more open to new things. Worship is one area where older adults can feel left behind. By creating opportunities for older adults to plan and participate in worship, no matter what their age, doors are opened to working with others on new ideas. Things such as flower arrangements or banner making may be sufficient for some people. Others may be persuaded to lead worship or even to reflect on some aspect of their life journey as part of the teaching or sermon.

Worship is about encountering God. The way we worship is very important to us. As we seek to make worship relevant to younger generations, let us also consider the older generations.

You can incorporate rituals or recognition for significant passage points in older age. Included in appendix C is a "ritual for leaving work" that could become an annual worship recognition of those who are retiring. You can recognize anniversaries of those achieving fifty, sixty, and seventy years of marriage. While Grandparents Sunday in September may seem like just another commercialized "Hallmark" holiday, perhaps you can recognize grandparents during a worship time. While one always needs to be careful not to leave out people with these types of recognitions, we need to create many opportunities to celebrate in the life of the congregation (and most people either retire, are grandparents, or have wedding anniversaries).

While many congregations involve older adults in lay leadership on any given Sunday, some older adults might be more inclined to take leadership in a special "gifts of older adults" worship service when their peers are also taking part.

**2. Belonging, hospitality, and fellowship.** As the story of Helen and Frank illustrated at the beginning of this chapter, some older adults have the gift of hospitality. Unleash this gift whenever possible. Hospitality offers a sense of well-being to both the giver and the receiver. It is a win-win situation. Older adults could serve as mentors for new parents as well. Older adults may be able to take disadvantaged parents and show them how to make good choices. Single parents might enjoy the company and caring conversation of an older adult who could help them face single parent life.

Also apparent in the opening story is the fact that older adults sometimes need to be welcomed back into their own congregations. Peer group events help older adults meet one another in new settings. Adopt-a-grandparent programs can link children to older adults. Helen enjoyed the variety of ages who cared for her. Ministry with older adults involving other generations adds variety and life.

A practical fellowship activity might be a special fellowship meal once a year celebrating the birthdays of all those eighty or ninety and above. Youth could put it on and serve it, or another group in the church.

Some congregations have elder fellowships that meet once a month or quarter, similar to youth fellowships. If your congregation is big enough, you may want to consider having a paid or volunteer senior pastor who helps plan activities and keeps senior agenda on the plate of the congregation.

**3. Serving God by serving others.** The importance of service and volunteering has already been well noted in this book, but we include it here as one of the four aspects of a well-rounded Christian life and congregation (worship, fellowship, mission or service, and nurture). Older adults may be eager to do works of service they could not do until now because of job and family obligations. Once again this can be a cross-generational experience, or there may be opportunities to meet and work with older adults from the same or different faith communities. One community tells the story of older adults showing up at the church early one morning to see the youth off on a week-long service project. The older adults prayed them onto the buses and promised to continue holding them in prayer all week.

As older adults become ill or homebound for other reasons, the congregation can take advantage of many ways to serve them. If congregational members visit to do chores around the house, it is important that time be set aside to simply visit. Caring conversation that builds trusting relationships is a key to ministry in all aspects, especially with older adults who do not have much contact with the outside world.

Mentoring is often the first suggestion to come to mind. Older adults can mentor across the generations. Developing a special relationship with a child, youth, or young adult can make a significant difference in mentor and mentee. Mentoring can mean helping a young adult get on their feet by offering advice and encouragement while walking with them through this intense part of life. What child would not appreciate a surrogate grandparent if the real ones are not present? The book *Tuesdays With Morrie*, by Mitch Albom, illustrates how profoundly an older, dying adult can affect the life of a middle-aged adult.

**4. Interpreting and understanding God's Word.** Bible study that is challenging can stimulate faith and promote thinking. Bible study and other book studies can stir the emotions, memories, and can call people to action. Bible study is one of the activities that older adults can engage in that provides a wide array of responses.

Older adults can also lead Bible studies or other nurture activities because of their experience, time to prepare, and in many cases, greater familiarity with the Bible. Preparing to lead a study always benefits the teacher the most; thus, taking leadership roles helps the older adult maintain an active and growing faith.

# CHAPTER 10

# Dying Well: How to Have a Good Death

By Pam Reese Comer

> There is a time for everything
>    and a season for every activity under heaven:
> A time to be born and a time to die,
> A time to plant and a time to uproot.
>    —Ecclesiastes 3:1-2

When I received the call to contribute to this book and was asked to write a chapter on a "good death," I instinctively agreed. This was my field, my area of expertise. I've worked with death, dying, loss, and grief issues going on twenty years now. This project would come naturally and as long as I had enough preparation time, it would flow easily. So I placed the project on the proverbial back burner until the calendar allotted me time to focus.

Then the focus came: how naïve of me to think a reflection on a good death would come easily or instinctively! Death is neither easy nor a basic instinct for human beings. We still live in a death-denying society despite all our efforts to the contrary. Much like that famous battery-run bunny—medical science, fitness gurus, health arenas, and yes, even some of our spiritual leaders—would keep us going and going and going. So the question becomes, just what is a "good death"? What does "dying well" mean?

Is it subjective with no avenue to consolidate one definition? Or is there a way to at least reflect on what having a good death might mean to us?

I think about all the people I've counseled or educated on loss. Would they all agree on one definition of a good death? No! Each of us bases our view of death on life, I suppose.

I am reminded of a courageous woman whom I will call Mary. She and I met when she was fifty-six, a wife, mother, and grandmother. She worked in education, had hobbies, friends, active church involvement, and most of the connections we all desire at that season of our life. She was in fairly good health and physically active. Her mother was still living but she had lost her father several years prior. She also had lost a cousin, aunt, and her favorite grandmother since she was forty-three. So she was no stranger to the fact of death or the experience of grief.

But one Tuesday afternoon, just an ordinary day, which is how it happens sometimes, she listened to her physician begin to describe a heart problem that required immediate treatment. I remember her describing in great detail the shock that she experienced as she began a long journey that she felt inadequately prepared for and that made her face issues she had avoided. She asked me, "How do we prepare for death when life is what we want, thrive on, and when we have no interest in letting go?"

Of course, I had no pat answer. It made me wonder also. How do we balance the fact of life and the fact of death in the very same human body and mind? How do we allow ourselves to prepare for a letting go when it is our human instinct to stay attached? Perhaps the key word is balance in understanding our nature and in accepting our mortality. It also may help to understand how our generations have arrived at our current state of mind where death is concerned.

*Perspective*

If you and I lived several centuries ago, our definition of a good death would be quite different. We would hope to live to our forties or fifties and not die of some sudden illness that today can be controlled by a simple antibiotic. Our family would care for us at home when we were ill. When we died at home, the town would come visit in our home while our body lay in the parlor. Children would have been involved in the entire experience and not sheltered as they are today. Our family would probably make the wooden box, dig the grave, and bury us at the funeral.

This is quite a different picture than the current one where we may or may not die at home and our family can pay for others to care for us, purchase a casket, and pay third parties to conduct our elaborate funeral. For most of us, death has changed from a first-hand experience to a second- or third-hand one in which we become observers and not active participants in the journey. Families are scattered all over and technology is able to sustain life and prolong death. We are not always able to care for someone completely at home like our ancestors. With death being more removed from us while we are growing up, by the time we are adults we may never have had a first-hand experience nor a look at death in an open manner. Then one day we are faced with a loss or our own mortality and we feel ill-equipped on an emotional level to process what we need to do on a practical level. With all this in mind, the key becomes educating yourself about how to prepare what you can and, at the very least, allowing yourself to consider the fact of your own death.

*Being prepared*

The following are considerations for being prepared for your death. Since each state may have different regulations, please check local resources for more specific information.

**1. Advance directive or living will.** This is a document stating your wishes that no life-prolonging measures be taken should you be unable to speak for yourself. It may include a living will form and a "power of attorney for healthcare needs" form. When you complete these forms, be as specific as you can. In other words, "I do not want to be hooked up to a ventilator, I do want to be fed intravenously, I do not want to be resuscitated should my heart stop." The more clear you are about your wishes, the easier you make it on whomever carries them out and the more you can be assured that they understand your wishes. Review the form with your physician and ask good questions. Most hospitals are required to offer you this opportunity when you come in for services. Check with your local hospital for a booklet. Go over this form with your family, your physician, and the person you designate as power of attorney for your healthcare needs. Remember that communication is the key. Your documents are only as good as the understanding of the people you expect to follow them. A copy of this document should be in your medical file at your physician's office and at your local hospital when you need services.

**2. Wills.** A will is a document stating how your assets will be distributed after your death. You may arrange this through your attorney. Many bookstores or office stores have kits you can purchase to guide you through the process. Remember not having a will means complicating matters for your family later on. Even if you are younger and think it is not necessary, it is a vital document to have secured for your children, spouse, or business. It's never too soon to have a will.

**3. Advance funeral planning.** If you've ever been involved in planning a funeral, you know the details and stress that people face during this traumatic time. Many funeral homes offer a preplanning service. You can meet with the funeral director ahead of time, explore options, and even pay for your own service in advance. Many people who know they are terminally ill choose this option to help their loved ones. But you can plan ahead even if you are healthy and file the information away with other important papers. Your wishes are recorded and your loved ones simply follow the plan. This can ease some of the tedious work for your family in the first days after your death. The key here is to make sure you go over the plan with whomever may be involved in planning your funeral or memorial service. Contact your local funeral home for more information. Even if you do not desire to go as far as working with a funeral home, you can keep a file (inform your family) listing your preference for arrangements after your death.

**4. Power of attorney (POA).** A power of attorney is a representative who will carry out your wishes should you become incapacitated.

> –Medical POA: This person is designated by you in a document and will work with medical professionals in stating your wishes. When choosing a POA for healthcare needs, choose a person you trust and who you talk to extensively about your wishes for treatment. Remember to communicate this information to your family and physician. Check with your local hospital or your attorney for this document.
>
> –Financial/Legal POA: This person manages your finances and may or may not be the same person you designate for healthcare needs. Again, choose someone you trust. You can arrange this document through your attorney.

### About family and friends

Beyond facing our own mortality, the most challenging aspect of even considering our death is the consideration of our loved ones. All the preparation in the world will not make them ready for the loss. If we can learn to approach death in an open manner, discussing our wishes with them and even sharing ideas, we may be able to lessen the practical load a bit, which in turn eases their stress when we die. Many families do not talk about death or teach their children until they are in the thick of a loss. Then our internal resources are at an all-time low. Depending on your season of life and on the medical conditions you face, you may want to consider providing your family opportunities to talk more openly about the realities of death, the hope you have from your faith, and questions or concerns they have for the future. Even if you are completely healthy, remember that talking more openly about death is a form of preparation in itself. Healthy families learn to embrace the endings in life as much as they embrace the beginnings.

The following are ways you can help your family deal more openly about death. How you use this as a guide may depend on the age and stage of your family.

**1. Use life experiences to create discussions on loss.** Pet deaths, other families' experiences, news stories, and trips to visit relatives in nursing homes can be good times to talk with your children or other family members about death and loss.

**2. When there is a death in the family, talk about the experience.** Mention the person's name. Reminisce about his or her life. Talk about your own thoughts and fears about death.

**3. Share your own wishes for funeral arrangements.** Be creative and encourage family input. If you have forms and lists, make sure members of your family know their location. Go over these with them. Once you do that task, they can sit in a file until needed. You may be surprised at what you teach your family by doing this important task.

**4. If humor plays a part in family talks on loss, let it be.** Humor is a natural coping mechanism for difficult topics—it lessens the tension. A dear friend of mine facing a life-threatening illness joked with her adult children about having all her shoes and hats at her memorial service since she had quite a collection. They joined in and suggested people try on her shoes and hats and wear them in the service. That family will never forget the precious moments sharing a laugh over something so scary and real. Pain and laughter can mix to provide a more balanced atmosphere.

**5. Take a spiritual journey of your own.** Review your life. Take inventory of what you have learned about yourself, others, and life in general. Write or tape your thoughts. Answer some questions for yourself: What has been most meaningful to me in my life? What will be the hardest to let go of when my death is near? What do I need to do to feel as prepared as possible?

### The difference is called hope

Putting the difficult task of preparation for our own death aside, there is an even more complex and deeper issue driving us. You would think that given the Christian belief system, death would be a celebration for us all. There would be no mourning after we go because we are with God. That should be the culmination of our religion, a reuniting with our Lord—a homegoing. If we know our death is near, such as in a cancer situation, you might think we are excited, ready, and willing to reunite with our Lord. While some people describe these experiences, there is also a stronger element playing a role here. We are humans, with human needs and desires. We are attached to this world and the people in it from birth. We spend our lives attached to people, relationships, dreams, goals, careers, and yes, material objects. So why would we be excited about leaving all we know as "home"? And therein lies the ambivalence to our earthly journey: the tug of war between life and death, between here and there, between being with our families here and being with God.

My own personal struggle with this dilemma came at the worst time of my life, after my best friend in the world died suddenly at the home we shared. I found her one Saturday morning when I casually walked down the steps anticipating a relaxing cup of coffee. From that moment my life took a permanent turn, never to be the same again. We were friends for more than seventeen years and shared a home for many of those. So she was a friend and a sister. Her absence in my daily routine and life in general was devastating.

I remember with great clarity the week I met this difference I call hope. It was about three months after her death and I had a full week ending with a two-day workshop I had to teach. I was exhausted. This business of death takes all your energy. It was Friday and the workshop was over at 4:30, but I had to go see a client at 5:00 who could not wait until Monday. I could feel the emotion building all week as I struggled to manage my obligations. I saw the client and then had to pick up a prescription for my sinus infection. Grieving can make your immune system weaker. I pulled into the pharmacy parking lot praying hard. The tears needed to come and I had one more thing to do before I could go home and have a good cry. I was struggling to hold the tears back. *Dear God, please help me. I am so weak and tired. I miss her so much. I ache. Please help me. Why did this happen? How could this be okay with you? I can't stand this. You've got to help me. What am I going to do?*

Then very clearly, a simple yet very strong statement came to me. This was a "knowing," if you will, from a place no one can misunderstand. A gentle but forceful *she's with me now* feeling came. I put the car in park and just sat there for a few minutes. The car and I came to a sudden stillness at the same time. It was the kind of stillness that you know will only last a few seconds but is life changing. I decided to process it after I was out of the pharmacy. I drove home in awe.

This is what the whole struggle is: she is with God and that is wonderful. She lives with God. The spirit in me rejoices in that, yet the human being in me wants her with me. That day brought me peace. But let me be clear about what I mean by peace. I do not mean I never wanted her back. I do not mean I never cried or grieved again. I mean that I released the struggle and accepted the journey, the ambivalence and the assurance of God's steadfast walk by my side in all my humanness of wanting her to be at peace with the Lord and with me all at the same time. This thing called hope makes it possible for us to have permission to both resent the fact of death and embrace the hope of the homegoing. I would suggest that we allow both to peacefully coexist in our struggles.

People who are close to death are only being honest when they say, "I am ready to go but I hate to leave my loved ones." For many Christians, it's not the dying that is the trouble, it's the leaving. What makes it possible for this struggle to be handled? What is the difference that allows us to survive this unsolvable issue that only our Lord fully understands?

The Scriptures present us with the reality of peace, assurance, and a sense that the act of death is a culmination of our journey here: "Now may the Lord of peace himself give you peace at all times and in every way" (2 Thessalonians 3:16). And, "If we live, we live to the

Lord; and if we die, we die to the Lord. So whether we live or die, we belong to the Lord" (Romans 14:8).

We belong to the Lord! Death is a return to our Lord and Maker. It must be like what we feel at the end of a long day of hard, rigorous work and demands that leaves us with weary bones, aching muscles, and a desire for rest. Then we are still, a sense of calm like no other. We are home. There's no place like home.

# CHAPTER 11

# Saying Good-bye

By Shirley Yoder Brubaker

> Why is it that we rejoice at a birth and grieve at a
> funeral?
> It is because we are not the person involved.
> —Mark Twain

*M*y family attended all the funerals in our congregation when I was a child. I remember the sadness that descended on me as our family entered the sanctuary and found a seat. We seldom sat together as a complete family except at funerals. When all were seated, the side door at the front of the sanctuary opened and the grieving family entered. Every eye was fastened on the family as if looking would send strength and comfort to each mourner.

Then the service began. Prayer, Scripture, congregational singing, an obituary chronicling the important dates of the deceased's life, a sermon, and always special music. Then the funeral director would slowly walk down the center aisle to the closed casket, open it, fuss with the lining, and then direct the congregation to file past. In slow cadence, as if marching to the inner echo of "Safe in the Arms of Jesus," we walked to the open casket. The silence would occasionally be punctuated with sobbing as someone expressed grief. I remember always tearing up, even if the deceased was eighty-one-year old Anna Nisly, whom I barely knew, or Lawrence Good, a thirty-something father of six, a logger killed by a falling tree. Someone who had always been in church was gone forever. And even though I couldn't grasp what "forever" meant, or understand about "death being swallowed up in victory," I did realize that this was a final parting and I would never, ever see this person again.

### Why have a funeral?

In most instances, the word funeral in this chapter can be replaced with memorial service. Today there is little differentiation between the two, although originally a memorial service usually meant the body was not present.

Death is part of our natural, created order. But death brings with it sorrow and grief, sometimes pain and suffering, occasionally trauma. None of us welcomes the loss of control we feel when experiencing grief. In fact, we have learned to minimize suffering and avoid the pain grief brings. But pain and suffering play important roles in our lives.

Our culture has grown to expect controlled grief at a funeral. We cringe at brokenhearted sobs and loud wails. But a funeral is the perfect place to sob and express the pain we feel at this wrenching loss. For one hour or so, we can concentrate our thoughts on our relationship with that one person and share those thoughts with others who also knew and loved him or her.

"How is Tom doing?" is one of our first questions after the death of Tom's wife. Why? Do we hope to spare ourselves the hard work of walking with someone through a messy emotional journey? Is it a painful reminder of our own mortality? The truth is, when someone we love dies, we will grieve. And we need something to help us deal with this new intruder, death, in our lives.

We have always used rituals in the church to help us

adapt to transitions that come in life. We dedicate our children to the Lord at their birth, we use water to baptize new members into the faith community, we eat and drink at the Lord's table, we may wash the feet of one another, we anoint the sick with oil, and at death, we gather to acknowledge our leave-taking of this life. Rituals are time-honored ways of dealing with change.

Alan D. Wolfelt, in *Creating Meaningful Funeral Ceremonies*, says: "Rich in history and rife with symbolism, the funeral ceremony helps us acknowledge the reality of the death, gives testimony to the life of the deceased, encourages the expression of grief in a way consistent with the culture's values, provides support to mourners, allows for the embracing of faith and beliefs about life and death, and offers continuity and hope for the living."

Not everyone in our generation appreciates or understands the importance of the funeral ritual. Grandparents, parents, aunts, and uncles are living into their eighties and nineties, so it is not rare to find middle-aged people who have not experienced the death of a close relative. More than once, a parishioner has asked whether there has to be a funeral. And always my answer has been, "Yes." Yes!

The ritual of a funeral ceremony can offer three gifts to us. First, it provides a link with the past. At the time of a death, everything is in upheaval. Nothing seems normal. We desperately need something that says, "Not everything is out of control." And a funeral can do that. It is a ritualized act that gives public shape to our grief. The familiarity of a traditional funeral service provides an accommodating groove that keeps careening emotions within safe boundaries.

Second, the ritual of a funeral ceremony makes the present real. We will never again see or speak to the one who has died. Someone who has been physically present with us is now gone forever and we need a ritual to assist us in moving from what was to what is. The routines at death—contacting a funeral home, planning the funeral service, viewing the body, and witnessing the casket lowered into the earth or scattering the ashes, force us to admit the finality of death.

A funeral gives us the opportunity to deal with the difficult questions that often come at death. Why did this good person die so young or so tragically? Why does it hurt so much? Why must we die? What happens after death? For people of faith, a meaningful funeral will provide comfort and invite and stretch our faith to welcome this stranger called Death into our lives. We willingly stand in the face of death in faith, not fear—in reality, not fantasy.

Third, the funeral moves us toward the future. What happens at the service will greatly affect how the bereaved go on to find meaning and purpose in continued living. When a grieving family walks into the sanctuary and sees it filled with relatives, friends, school classmates of the children, and neighbors, they immediately feel uplifted by the emotional and spiritual support the attendees represent. By having a public funeral, a family is asking, "Come, support us. Help us move on." And by attending, we as family and friends are answering, "We will give you support, compassion, hope, and understanding." It is the beginning of a healthy journey through the stages of grief.

From now on we will relate to each in new roles, for we have never been together before without the deceased. A funeral is a safe social environment to try on this new role that we will wear for the rest of our lives together.

### *Looking at the biblical text*

In Ecclesiastes we read: "It is better to go to a house of mourning than to go to a house of feasting, for death is the destiny of every man; the living should take this to heart. Sorrow is better than laughter, because a sad face is good for the heart" (Ecclesiastes 7:2-3).

Why does the teacher, as the speaker in Ecclesiastes is called, think the opposite of what we normally think? Most of us would much prefer a festive event to a funeral. The teacher seems to be suggesting that attending a funeral is more significant because it is something we all have to do at some time, even if it is just our own. Feasts and parties are not events we have to attend, and besides, they happen only occasionally.

We think about things when we attend a funeral that never cross our minds when we are partying. "The living should take this to heart" suggests that those thoughts are sober thoughts about the meaning of life and our own demise. There is something about grief that is good for the heart (mind) because it makes us come to terms with our own mortality.

The joy and happiness of a feast or wedding or party seldom make us contemplate such serious thoughts. Instead, we are full of ideas and hopes for the future— who the newborn will grow up to be, the beginning of a long marriage for the newlyweds, a promising career facing the graduate.

It is not morbid to muse on our own death or what we want our funeral to be like. Doing so, while it may create sadness, will also bring joy because of what we know our future in Christ to be.

### At the time of death

Saying good-bye to a loved one actually begins well before a planned funeral service—at the time of death. Sometimes there is opportunity for family who are present to spend time with the person who has died, even before an undertaker or other helper is called. As a pastor, I have some suggestions for making this time meaningful and special, since many are thrust into this situation without having any idea of what to do immediately after someone has died.

- Take a few minutes for silence, prayer, or song. Gather in silence for a few moments, perhaps holding hands or touching the body together. Words are not necessary for a gesture to have meaning. What is important is to find the appropriate level of comfort and participation for each. Each family member could be given private time with the body before it is transferred to the funeral home, then all can join for a joint farewell. A blessing can be given. If a pastor is present at the passing, he or she would be happy to lead in this brief ritual.

- Sometimes people outside the immediate family are present when a loved one dies. If they do not remove themselves so family can have a private time with the body, simply invite them to wait in the hall while you say your good-byes. (Not all visitors have common sense!) If death occurs in a hospital, the nursing staff will need to be informed. They have several tasks they do with a body and then family is free to say their private good-byes. It is also acceptable to say the good-byes before informing the nursing staff.

### Planning the funeral service

As plans progress, the family is often thrown into emotional upheaval. Making decisions becomes difficult. Each of us can help our family by planning ahead for our own funeral and letting them know what we would like at a funeral service. By our doing so, our families will need to make fewer decisions at a time when they are least able to make them. Never extract promises from your family to carry out your wishes exactly. For any variety of reasons, family may not be able to honor your desires and the last thing family needs at the time of your death is guilt. Your preplanning is a guide, not a set of rules.

A funeral should honor the person who died while giving the family an opportunity to celebrate a life and mourn a death. Because our culture tends to squelch wild grief, we find it easy to plan funerals that celebrate someone's life, but avoid moments that allow the tears to flow. At a funeral we gather to honor and remember the person who has died, and we gather to receive God's hope, comfort, and inspiration at a time of great sorrow.

Most funerals are similar in structure—music, prayer, eulogy, Scripture, and a meditation. They are most meaningful when each element is personalized for the person who died. Just as no two people are alike, so should no two funerals be alike.

Since a Christian funeral is usually done inside the church the deceased has been associated with, perhaps the duties of the funeral director should end and begin at the door of the church. Having strangers conduct the funeral inside the church is adding unreality to a situation that needs a healthy dose of reality and familiarity. Use congregational ushers and greeters to seat people and help at the guest book, let the pastor or worship leader assist with preparations for viewing, invite pallbearers to actually bear the casket rather than trail behind the professionals. Certainly the funeral home personnel can bring the casket to the door of the church and then receive it there again at the close of the service.

### Opening remarks

The first words set the tone for the service, name the person we have gathered to remember, acknowledge the circumstances of how someone died, ask God's comfort, and perhaps express our corporate grief in song. The words that open a service define the space as holy and the time as sacred. Often grieving families find entering the sanctuary somewhat traumatic, so one question I have asked is, "What do you need at the beginning of the service?" God's comfort? Then we will begin with a prayer or Scripture. The love and support of your friends? Then we will begin with a song. Silence to gather yourself emotionally? Then we will invite the congregation to silence. One grieving family, planning the funeral of a murdered daughter, answered that question without hesitation. "Something from Bach." So, without words, after the family had taken their seats, the organist played a wonderful Bach prelude. All of us gathered strength from the musical interlude so we could continue a grievous journey together.

If the funeral is for someone who has died by suicide, that needs to be named early on in the service. Naming suicide defuses its power over the emotions and the service itself. To not speak of what everyone already knows casts a shadow of unreality over a service that is to help us face reality.

### *Honoring and remembering the person who died*

While many of the elements in a funeral honor the deceased in some way, the eulogy, a "portrait in words," is specifically dedicated to this. This portrait will acknowledge the uniqueness of this person and affirm the significance of that life to those gathered. A eulogy is more than an obituary, more than a string of biographical data. Certainly it includes the facts of their life—date of birth, names of children, occupation, date of death. But it contains so much more—anecdotes and stories, quotes from family and friends, hobbies and activities that gave his or her life meaning. An obituary is what appears in the newspaper; it is not what is read at a funeral. One of my worst funeral memories is of a grandson reading his grandfather's obituary verbatim at the funeral, never changing "Mr. Yoder" to "Grandpa." The person we had gathered to remember never came alive to us in that service.

The portrait eulogy can be difficult to do if the person who died had glaring faults. Truth is important at death, too, so since none of us is perfect, our eulogies should not picture us as such. If the deceased left painful memories for some, then the portrait eulogy may give a more complete story of who this complex person was. Don't forget the importance of humor. We often think of laughing and crying as opposite ends of a straight-line continuum. But pick up those ends and bring them together in a circle. How close these two emotional outlets are. That's why laughing so frequently turns into crying and vice versa. They do the same therapeutic work.

Tributes from family and friends also enlarge our memory of the deceased. Practices differ from congregation to congregation whether the tributes are assigned or spontaneous. If assigned, listen carefully to whether someone feels they can do so emotionally. If spontaneous, have some tolerance for the unpredictable. All of us have horror stories of someone who went on and on, or shared something inappropriate, or spoke more about themselves than the deceased. Many congregations save the spontaneous tributes for the mealtime that often follows the funeral.

Other ways to honor the person who has died include favorite Scripture and music, quoting from their own writings, a "show and tell" of their handiwork, or a memorial program booklet.

***Bringing God's hope, comfort, and strength***

Meditation, Scripture, prayer, and music can all bring us into God's presence. A meditation should reflect the life of the person who has died. We do not come to a funeral to be evangelized or philosophize about death. We come to mourn and reflect on the meaning of life and to receive comfort and strength to continue life without the one who has died. We come to be reminded that death is not the final victor, that love will triumph, that eternal life is the hope of all who believe.

***Committal and burial***

This brief service at the graveside symbolizes the final separation from the person we love. Usually there is Scripture, prayer, and perhaps a song. All remind us of the return to God, the giver and source of life. In recent years, families have sometimes opted not to have a committal service. Again, it feels like an avoidance of the pain associated with assigning the body back to the earth from which it came. At the same time, other families are returning to earlier practices that involved families in the burial of the body—helping to lower the casket into the ground, throwing handfuls of dirt onto the casket, or helping to shovel dirt into the grave.

Committal deals with the remains of the body, whether embalmed or cremated. Most often it will immediately precede or follow a funeral or memorial service. Occasionally, it is separated from the funeral or memorial service when the family can gather together only at a later date.

Families have become much more creative about the committal service. Since the body is returning to the earth from which it is made, celebrate the basic elements of life—earth, air, fire, water. Plant a tree or flower bulbs, release butterflies into the air, scatter flowers into the grave, release ashes into a stream, or place significant objects in the grave to also return to dust.

Do remember that burial of a body or ashes must meet state or local regulations. Burying Grandpa under the oak tree in the back pasture might not be allowed. A body does not need to be embalmed if buried within a specified time, but again, there are some strict regulations about this. The funeral director will know what these regulations are for your area.

### Costs

Those of us who frequently work with funerals would agree that they can be far too expensive. Because families need to make so many decisions at a time when least emotionally able to think clearly, they do not always make the wise decisions of a good steward. Families need to live within their means and make choices that reflect their values. Choose less expensive caskets or have members of the family skilled in woodworking create a casket. A spray of funeral flowers for the top of the casket is in the $150 range. If the deceased was a farmer, how about a handful of wheat instead? If a gardener, a bouquet of flowers from his or her garden? Being creative is an act of loving remembrance. A funeral or memorial service does not need to be lavishly expensive to be meaningful. And remember, cremation is less expensive.

Trinity Mennonite Church in Glendale, Arizona, has purchased a common casket to help families avoid some of the expense of a funeral. Another congregation has purchased a pall, a heavy cloth used to cover a casket, so all appear the same—from expensive walnut to pine box.

### Cremation

Cremation is much more accepted now than in the past. Those who choose cremation often do so because that reflects best their values about life and death, the environment, or stewardship. If the deceased is to be cremated, who makes that decision is often problematic. What if the person who has died requested cremation, but the surviving spouse does not agree? What if the family wants cremation, but the deceased has never made his or her wishes known?

For families who choose cremation, the survivors should make the final decision about the disposition of the ashes. For some, burial of the ashes is important for they need a physical site where they can gather in remembrance. For others, choosing a place to strew the ashes is a healing process for it honors the loved one. One family I worked with chose three places important to the father—his outdoor workplace, his sons' Little League playground, and the churchyard. The immediate family participated in the final disposal of the ashes.

One additional decision for families who choose cremation is whether to include the urn of ashes in the funeral or memorial service. When the vase is included, often it is simply placed on the front table in the sanctuary. It can be placed there prior to the beginning of the service, or a family member can carry it in and place it there when the family processes in at the beginning of the service.

### Including children

Perhaps we need to first reflect on the reasons we as adults want to protect children from experiencing death. Children will have far more fears about death if they *don't* experience the rituals and traditions than if they do. The unknown is always more frightening than the known. What better place is there for them to begin their experience of death than within the faith community? The familiar faces of a pastor, Sunday school teachers and classmates, and family friends will not only expose them to the love and care of friends, but will also give a human face to the love and care of God.

Children need to know what to expect before they attend a funeral. Tell them exactly what will be happening and why. If a body will be viewed, let them know that ahead of time and let them choose whether to look. Children can understand that people will be sad at a funeral because someone has died and we will never see them again or hear them talk or play with them. If the deceased is a close family member or a friend, invite them to express their sorrow in a tangible way. Perhaps they can place a memento in the casket, or share a memory, or draw a picture to give to someone, or light a candle.

Children will be children even if the deceased is a parent or sibling. They do not remain in grief as adults do. They will break from their grieving to play a game or watch a video or roughhouse with a friend. Don't stop them by saying, "You shouldn't be doing that. Your daddy just died." One way in which young children express their feelings is through play. So expect a child to play "funeral" for a while—decorating a box as a casket and placing a doll inside, pretending to cry, conducting a funeral service, and even burying the casket. (Don't worry. They'll dig it up later to retrieve the doll!) When my sister's family met at the funeral home for the first viewing of her grandson's body, she gathered the four surviving grandchildren around her and read a story to them which explained death from a child's perspective. One such book is *Water, Bugs, and Dragonflies* by Doris Stickney. Then the grandchildren were invited to see Daniel in his casket. Not all wanted to do so at first. But eventually each did.

### Viewing the body

In many communities, the body is no longer viewed at a funeral service. Somehow that practice has become something unseemly. Yet viewing the body is a reality check. Even though our mind refuses to believe that someone has died, it is true, and viewing the body forces our mind to begin to accept the fact that the loved one is truly gone. To see the body invites us to say our farewells to someone we loved. It is not morbid or a sideshow at the state fair. The open casket can be placed in a classroom, fellowship hall, library, or nave so that people coming to the funeral can choose whether to view the body.

### If there is a step-family

One last word about an issue that is involved more and more in funeral planning. Most families anymore include step-families or former spouses or second spouses. Often these family members feel left out in the planning and carrying out of a service, even if it isn't an intentional act on the part of the biological family. Where do they sit at the funeral? With the family? The same is true if the family includes someone with a partner of the same sex or an unmarried partner. A funeral is not a time or place to exclude those family members whose moral behaviors we might not condone. Grief does not honor those kinds of boundaries. A son living with a woman without benefit of marriage grieves as much for the death of his mother as a son who has been married for twenty years.

If your family is a conflicted family, those imperfections will emerge as a funeral service is planned. Acknowledge the conflict by choosing a minister or location that does not identify with a particular side of the family. If alienation within the family is so severe that funeral planning is stalled, consider seeking the presence of a counselor or mediator when planning the funeral. Emotions are so raw at the time of death that even normal family differences can be exacerbated.

# CHAPTER 12

# A Toolkit for Aging and Loving It

By Ann Bender

> I now contemplate the approach of the moment
> of my retirement with the fondness of a sailor
> who has land in view.
> —Thomas Jefferson

*M*ost of us do not think about aging until we begin thinking about retirement. We actually begin the process of aging at the time of conception. How we deal with the time when we do become conscious of the aging process has a lot to do with how we live our lives.

People who live in one geographical area of the country may deal with the process of aging differently than those who have lived in a number of locations throughout the country or in other world cultures. Married people think of it differently than single people. People who continue to stretch their minds, whether through formal or informal education, think about aging differently. As we become more informed and more mobile, expectations related to aging may change. We become less attached to one geographical location. Many of us leave the workplace healthier today, with more information and financial resources than in earlier times. Today's market finds the resources of retirees delightful as they develop more and more living options for more adventurous retirees. Expectations are constantly being raised as options increase.

How do we prepare ourselves for the years after we leave the full-time career world? How do we walk into that world with a toolkit that allows us to continue this dynamic aging process successfully? And how can we make sure we love it? Does it have something to do with how much we love life before we move into this transition? An unknown author said, "We get more like we always were." Perhaps we should be made aware of this early in life.

Someone once said "It is good to have a book to guide you as your raise your children. But you will need a different book for each child." The same is true of older adults. We are all different. Therefore it is equally difficult to develop one formula for aging that fits all.

So how do we develop a toolkit for aging that will fit all? Furthermore we are implying that if you use this toolkit, you will love aging. First of all, not many people admit they love aging. Why not? We have been programmed to view the process of aging negatively. Although the media are changing, we still see many images of older people that depict them negatively. They are often seen as making silly, stupid mistakes and as the laughingstock of younger people. Or they may be seen as crotchety and sick. If they become ill, it is seen as the simple result of age.

Indeed there are people with health problems who can no longer take care of the activities of daily living. Approximately 30 percent retire with incomes below $25,000 a year and a smaller percent have incomes below the poverty level (approximately $10,000 a year). If we live past eighty-five we are much more vulnerable to these conditions. But this is a small percentage compared to the 75 or 80 percent who live with good health and who, in spite of limited incomes, manage their lives well. Many older adults with health problems remain optimistic and enjoy life in spite of physical limitations.

So how do we assemble the tools for a kit that will last us the rest of our lives? I will suggest tools that are cumulative, tools we have from the first fifty years of life, and tools that we can gather in anticipation of the next fifty-year journey. You may find some others to add to this list.

## The Toolkit

### *Happiness*

A relative recently said, "Your grandchildren are three of the happiest children I have ever seen." Goethe said, "Age does not make us childish, as they say. It only finds us true children still."

What makes children happy? Perhaps they are happy because no one has taught them not to be happy. So often we lose our ability to be creative and spontaneous in those early years because we are taught to simply fit in with others. Maybe our educational system is responsible for some of that. Children also need to be around adults who are happy, adults who have practiced being happy.

I have a wonderful friend who is in her nineties. Even when in pain, she is always positive. I believe she has practiced discovering what is good about living, although she once said with a grin, "Aging isn't what it's cracked up to be." She surrounds herself with reading material, including *The Washington Post,* paint and brush, and writing materials that she uses to write poetry. She sits in a large armchair with her telephone by her side, not moving a great deal due to severe osteoporosis. This woman earned a Ph.D. at age sixty and has traveled across continents. Now she and her husband, who learned to ski at age seventy, are confined to their house, a renovated log cabin. I still find them an inspiration. Somehow I believe they practiced being happy with whatever situation God gives them.

### A positive self-image

Becoming aware of our own strengths and personal value is sometimes hard to discuss. Those of us growing up in the Anabaptist tradition were taught the value of humility and were taught not to feel proud of our accomplishments. It certainly is hurtful if we make others feel less than important in God's eyes. Helping people around us identify their gifts can strengthen our ability to feel good about ourselves.

Some years ago I sat with a friend who was dying of cancer. Over and over she whispered the words, "Did I do a good job? Have I been a good mother?" I could only try to reassure her she had done well. When Jesus said, "Love your neighbor as yourself," surely he did not mean for us to hate ourselves. Otherwise how could we learn to love our neighbors? In fact, when a lawyer asked Jesus, "Which is the greatest commandment in the law?" he answered: "Love the Lord your God with all your heart and with all your soul and with all your mind. . . . And the second is like it, 'Love your neighbor as yourself.' All the Law and the Prophets hang on these two commandments" (Matthew 22:34-40).

### Continue to learn

The Lifelong Learning programs, an extension of Elderhostel, have provided many opportunities for older people to continue with formal education. People with limited incomes can frequently apply for scholarships to help pay for travel and other expenses.

Recent researchers have found that the older brain learns well and has the capacity to change. In a 2002 article in *Modern Maturity*, Richard Restak, M.D., writes, "New research shows that what you thought about the aging brain is all wrong. If we think the brain is always going down hill, we must be prepared for a surprise because they have learned that our brains have the capacity to change no matter what our age." Only when attacked by such diseases as Parkinson's and Alzheimer's are abstract thinking and verbal expression reversed. He and other researchers say that older people hold a clear advantage over younger minds because they have the ability to put things in context and reach a good decision with less information—otherwise known as wisdom. Older people may process information a bit more slowly but lack of speed is more than made up for by the knowledge we have accumulated over the years. This same article also offered ways to boost our brain power through physical exercise which pumps more blood to the brain, getting enough sleep, lessening stress by taking control of our lives, and supplementing our diet with B and E vitamins. The exceptions, of course are the health problems that may interfere with progress. They suggest that the older brain, however, learns to compensate just like we learn to use two hands to pick up a heavy object instead of one. Many older adults learn to compensate for limitations that may come with age, which allows them to live independently.

### Reach out—become a volunteer

Many friendships have been developed through organized volunteer activities covered in chapter 5. Much of the volunteer work older adults do is related to the church. Most often we tend to volunteer for jobs that lead us to other parts of the country. Why not see if our local congregations might use our talents? At a seminar on aging, a group of Christians discussed how we might better use the talents of older adults. Someone suggested that it would feel better if our congregations would ask us to take certain roles instead of expecting us to volunteer. I remember talking with an older woman in my congregation some years ago. She had been a Sunday school teacher and it seems she began to forget when it was her turn to teach so they took her off the list. Her response was, "They decided to put me on the shelf." Instead, couldn't we make a special effort to make sure she remembered?

In a "Pontius Puddle" cartoon, cartoonist Joel Kauffman, ponders: "We elderly have spent years planting seeds of faith, watering roots of belief, and cultivating spiritual gifts. So we asked the church to use us in a way that shows their respect for the elderly as a resource. And someone asked, 'What did they ask you to do? Teach? Counsel?' The reply: 'Weed flowerbeds.'"

### Cultivate friendships

Most of us have some special friends. For some it is easy to cultivate new friendships. But there are differences in the way we relate to each other. Siblings may or may not have developed mutual trust. Family members move to distant parts of the country because of career opportunities. Vance Packard, in *A Nation of Strangers*, discusses the problems we have developed in our country due to the mobility of families. It seems that people who move around a lot tend not to develop friendships and trust in others. They learn to be more anonymous, which he contends contributes to high crime rates. However, even when family members live in the same neighborhood they don't always cultivate close relationships. Distance does not necessarily preclude good relationships among families. The use of e-mail may even enhance communication among families.

When my parents needed assistance from their children, three out of four lived in other states. By using e-mail and telephone communication we were able to stay in touch with each other, reporting to each other as we took turns visiting with them on weekends.

As we get older we may lose some of our closest friends. It is important that we find ways to continue to relate to people with whom we have much in common even if we have to take the initiative to get to know them.

As a "retired person," I have found developing friendships with younger adults whom I have learned to know through volunteer opportunities to be very enriching. The energy and enthusiasm they exhibit is exciting even if I can't keep up with them. Often they are able to use the talents and time of older adults in meaningful partnership arrangements in the community.

Older homeowners in some communities have found a way to share the space in their homes with peers they trust. The house rich but cash poor homeowner may find a large house difficult to maintain. Although it takes careful matching skills, there are people who can live compatibly in a house together in assigned space. It is suggested that property maintenance, housekeeping, cooking, and other chores be done by someone who is paid instead of sharing these jobs among residents. This avoids possible conflicts over lifelong housekeeping and cooking skills. "Shared homes" have not become widely popular, but for some it is a way of sharing expenses and making it possible for older people with fixed incomes to live independently. Perhaps more should be encouraged to consider it.

### A sense of humor

I will always remember Moses Slabaugh when I talk about humor. Moses undoubtedly used humor in the most creative way. He once told me he went to the doctor because he had a sore knee. The doctor told him the pain was due to old age. He responded by telling the doctor his other knee was the same age and it didn't hurt at all. Moses wrote for the magazine *Christian Living* and other church publications well into his late eighties and also preached sermons.

In an article entitled, "Laughter, Nature's Medicine" in the magazine *Signs of the Time*, Elizabeth Johnson says, "Whether you have a cold or cancer, laughter can be an inexpensive, enjoyable ally on the road to recovery. . . . More and more the medical world is recognizing the healing qualities of plain, old-fashioned laughter— nature's doctor." Dr. William Fry of Stanford University (in the same article) says, "Laughter causes the muscles in the abdomen, chest, and shoulders to contract, the heart rate and pulse to increase, and you have stationary jogging."

Laughter can also be a therapeutic experience for both the patient and caregiver. Janette Adasiak, a registered nurse, in *Alzheimer's Caregiver,* writes that humor can provide relief from the psychological burdens of caregiver. It helps to relieve the patient from embarrassment and the memory of humor may influence how the patient acts in the future.

And how about humor as we go through the process of downsizing our living space and possessions? Consider this excerpt from Marj Arnoult's poem, "Worldly Goods."

I'm giving away my things and it turns out to be
As much of an occupation and as much fun as
   collecting them was.
I browse among my friends the way I used to
   browse in shops. . . .

*Toward a vision for including all elders*

As we prepare for a country with twice as many people over age sixty within the next twenty to thirty years, we may see this as either a problem or a challenge. Every day 5,422 people celebrate their sixty-fifth birthdays. Older women outnumber older men (20.5 million to 14.3 million). About 31 percent of non-institutionalized older people live alone. By the year 2030 we will have seventy million people over age sixty-five. The number over eighty-five years old will more than double. Members of minority groups will represent 25 percent of the older population by 2030, up from 16 percent now. In 1999, the median annual income of older men was $19,079 and for women, $10,943. According to the Social Security Administration, 90 percent reported that their major source of income was Social Security.

As Anabaptists, we may see this as a problem or a challenge. Our challenge will be to match each person with the opportunity to choose where they want to live. Most older people want to stay in their own homes. Most want to be in control of their own lives and make their own decisions. Most families are committed to taking care of their own family members and have a great deal of respect for their elderly relatives. And in most cases it is less expensive to live in your own home, unless you need twenty-four-hour nursing care.

The longer we live, the more likely our need for some kind of assistance to continue living at home. It is also likely that the buying power of our resources will not be as great as the day we retire. Assistance through some public or private source may be needed to continue to live independently with some acceptable quality of life.

Churches have the opportunity to work toward treating all elderly around us as sisters and brothers. For each of us, being included in family, our faith community, and local community is intertwined. We succeed or fail together. Jesus walked intimately with his family. He wept when his friend, Lazarus, died. He asked his disciple, John, to care for his mother, and wept over Jerusalem.

In 1965 Congress enacted the Older Americans Act to establish a national network of agencies to provide services that would enable elderly to maintain their independence in their home communities. For more than thirty years, 655 Area Agencies on Aging (AAAs), funded through this program have worked cooperatively with faith communities, civic groups, and private business to implement a variety of programs such as Meals on Wheels, personal care services, homemaker services, chore services, adult daycare, respite care, senior center programs, telephone reassurance, home repairs, and transportation. Through community collaboration, congregate meal programs have brought people together for recreational and educational opportunities. To protect the basic rights of the most vulnerable elderly who live in institutional settings, the long-term care ombudsman program was established.

Appendix E lists major resources that provide information about national programs. In addition, **The ElderCare Locator**, a service of the U.S. Administration on Aging, was established in 1991. The National Association of Area Agencies on Aging (N4A) administers a toll-free number (1-800-677-1116) that provides information and referral services offered by local agencies on aging, identified by every ZIP Code in the country. N4A can also be contacted through their website: www.n4a.org. This organization provides a link to services anywhere in the U.S.

Services will be similar all over the country. However, many communities depend heavily on volunteers, so there may be some differences in availability depending on your location. Peer counseling, for instance has been developed through funding from the Health Care Finance Administration to assist people with Medicare claims, supplemental, and long-term care insurance choices and claims.

All states have a program similar to what in Virginia is called the **Virginia Insurance Counseling and Assistance Program** (VICAP). Helping older people understand their Medicare claims has also helped the program identify fraud. This has saved the Medicare program millions by reporting suspicious claims.

**The National Caregiver Program** (NFCA), funded through the Administration on Aging, is a more recent program. Family caregiving has become a challenging issue. According to the NFCA, more than one quarter (26.6 percent) of the adult population has provided care to a family member or friend during the past year.

**Resources For Caregivers** is a comprehensive list of resources from N4A and can be accessed by calling 1-202-296-8130 or going to their website (www.n4a.org).

### *Your Personal Toolkit*

My hope is that every congregation will help individuals and their families personalize a toolkit for aging. Each congregation could develop a team—a medical professional, a social worker, at least one consumer or older person, and a caregiver. One of their projects should be to develop a resource file or information packet for each older person and their caregivers, leading them to resources that will enable them to live as independently as possible.

I believe it is consistent with our Christian heritage to support living in our own homes and communities as long as possible and appropriate. We have supported and put a lot of our financial resources into the development of retirement communities for our members and people from many other faiths who appreciate the quality of life provided on continuing care community campuses. Many older adults, however, do not have the resources to support living in such a community. Others prefer to stay in their own homes. Through partnerships with community resources and the development of volunteer and low-cost networks, I believe, we can continue to support our Christian heritage of community.

# Leader's Guide

### Settings for using this study

This curriculum is well suited for a study by a small group, Sunday school class, women's or men's group, summer intergenerational Sunday school class, week-long special study, or even a church retreat.

### Materials

We recommend buying or borrowing enough books for each household from a resource library, or enough to share so that all members can read materials between group sessions. Specific materials related to each chapter are listed under the chapter headings below. Only one video is needed per group, to be used in the group setting.

### Recommended ages

We recommend adults ages forty and up, but additional advantages and perspectives will be gained with positive benefit for the whole congregation when intergenerational groups study the materials together. The study is also ideal for small groups, including ones where there are children. There are suggested activities for use with children (usually ages five and up) sprinkled throughout. If an older Sunday school class wishes to study this topic, why not invite a class of younger adults to join you for the duration of the study?

## Time frame

**Full thirteen weeks:** There are twelve chapters in this book, which makes an excellent thirteen-week quarter (allowing one week for an introductory or wrap-up session). Or, take two weeks to study the two parts of chapter six or any other chapter where extra time is desired. Or, perhaps one class period might be given to a field trip to an area nursing home, funeral home, or other facility the group wants to visit. Chapter 12 does not include study questions but can be used as a time to do general discussion about the study or to pick up questions that you didn't get to in earlier sessions.

Most sessions can be accomplished in an hour or less. Using the additional learning activities or suggested field trips will expand the time of course.

**Six-week study:** For a quicker pace or more of an overview, take two chapters a week, eliminating about half of the study questions for each chapter.

## Use of video

Nine of the chapters have discussion starter segments on the videotape available with the book. In most cases, it is suggested you start the session with the video segment in order to jumpstart discussion, but it can be used whenever you see fit.

Always preview video segments before class so you will not be caught by surprise. Cue up the videotape to the correct segment so you won't have to waste class time looking for the segment. Feel free to stop and start or replay a segment as desired by the class. Note that the video is close-captioned and if you have any hearing issues in the group, you might want to play it so the captioning can be viewed to make "hearing" easier for all.

Make sure your monitor is big enough for the size of your group: the standard rule of thumb is if you have more than twenty-five people, you need at least two large monitors, nineteen inches or preferably more. If using the video for a large group or in a weekend retreat setting, consider renting or borrowing a video projector.

Use your own creativity to find or tape discussion starters

from TV or the library on selected topics if you desire more video segments for your group.

The companion video is available from Herald Press: 1-800-245-7894, and from Mennonite Media, 1-800-999-3534.

### Study questions

These are listed under their specific chapters. As the leader, you should determine which and how many of the study questions you wish to use. We tried to give you more than you will need so you can pick and choose for your group.

### Intergenerational group

Questions and activities that are especially well suited for groups that include children are highlighted with a **Child-friendly activity** tagline. There are more activities in appendix B as well. Some of the child-friendly activities are suitable for adults, even when children are not involved.

### Scripture lessons

Each chapter includes scriptural references for you to highlight as desired in your study. This section of your study can be expanded as appropriate for your group. For a more traditional Bible study or Sunday school class, you will want to spend time preparing and engaging in the text. Some of the chapters include study questions on the scriptural text.

### Use of learning exercises (see appendix B)

Appendix B contains ten different exercises involving extended discussion, experiential learning, field trips, or guest speakers. You will want to plan ahead to implement any of them as fits your group and schedule, and these are especially helpful when using this study in intergenerational groups or retreats. (Some activities, however, are designed only for adult groups.) There is a suggestion with each item as to which chapter the exercise goes with, but feel free to move them around as needed for your group's experience.

## Chapter 1: The Time of Our Lives

### Study questions

1. Are you in denial about your aging? Why or why not?

2. Have you ever lied about your age? Have you ever been tempted to lie?

3. How do you feel about products that make you look younger? What about dying hair, plastic surgery, body toners? Are these just matters of personal taste, or are they related to ageism in society?

4. How much of aging well or poorly is related to attitude? How much does it have to do with your health and how you feel?

5. How long would you like to live? Or are there other more important questions than how long you want to live?

6. Do you think there are gender differences in how people age? Discuss.

7. Share examples or stories of wisdom from older people, like the example of Aunt Susie in this chapter.

8. Are there young people in your congregation that you could encourage in the direction of a ministry or career in gerontology?

### Video segment study questions

(View segment 1: "The Time of Our Lives")

1. Do you think the "tsunami of caregiving" that Ira Byock talks about will happen? Why or why not? Do you think it will be experienced any differently in the church community?

2. How have you already experienced caregiving issues?

3. What do you think of the idea that we have to "get over it" to cope better with the reality of aging and dying in our lives? How would that help give us a happier life?

## Chapter 2: What Happens As We Grow Old

### Study questions

1. What individuals come to mind who, like Sister Green, represent a wholesome view of aging from your perspective?

2. What are some examples of "ageism" of which you are aware or have experienced personally?

3. Nine myths of aging are listed in this chapter. Which of these myths have you accepted at one time or another in your life? Which have you encountered?

4. How do you respond to the idea of aging as a process of growth, engagement, and integration?

5. What are some of the losses you anticipate (or have already experienced) as you age?

6. What are some of the gains that come with aging which you may not have been aware of before?

7. Which of the five developmental tasks seems especially challenging for you? Why?

8. Identify "little losses" you have experienced through life.

### Video segment study questions

(View segment 2: "What Happens As We Grow Old")

1. Have each group member tell one story from their growing up days. If the group is large, appoint the three oldest members as the storytellers.

2. Does anyone remember a time when an older person seemed to be happy to share their story? Tell about it.

3. What does storytelling at a funeral do for the survivors?

4. **Child-friendly activity.** If children are present, have them watch "The Box," a story of deaf children in Jamaica, to help them absorb a little of the flavor of Sister Green's spirit and country. (Found on the children's video, *Rhythms of Peace Around the World,* available from Mennonite Media, 1-800-999-3534.) Then have them talk about some of their favorite older people. Why are they

favorites? Tell them the story about meeting Sister Green
from the first part of this chapter. Have they ever been
lifted up by an older person? Who? Do they like it? Why
or why not? Children can also discuss what gifts (as symbolized by the box in the video) they have received from
grandparents and older people. What gifts can they, the
children, give back?

5. **Child-friendly activity.** Have older children or youth
   videotape older members of the congregations telling
   their stories. Then, watch the stories as a group.

### References and resources

Dychtwald, Ken and Joe Flower. *Age Wave: The Challenge and
Opportunities of an Aging America.* Los Angeles:
J. P. Tarcher, 1989.

Wolfe, David. *Serving the Ageless Market.* New York: McGraw-
Hill, 1990.

## Chapter 3: What the Body Says

### Study questions

1. What images do you have from movies and television
   programs that affect how you view the process of growing older? Reflect on movies such as *The Old Man and the
   Sea, Fried Green Tomatoes, On Golden Pond, Driving Miss
   Daisy, Grumpy Old Men,* etc.

2. Reflect on television programs such as "The Golden
   Girls." Which character do you most closely identify with,
   and why? If there were a series depicting four men of the
   same ages, what stereotypes would likely be portrayed?

3. What Scripture passages come to mind as you read this
   chapter? What are the images of aging that are relayed?

4. What information in this chapter did you find reassur-
   ing? What information produced anxiety and why?

5. What questions do you have about normal age changes? List these questions. Then as a group, identify sources of accurate information that can provide answers to the questions.

6. **Child-friendly activity.** During the week collect examples of TV and magazine advertisements that depict older adults. What products are being marketed, and for what implied "problems of old age"? Or, children could cut out images during class and create collages.

### *Video segment study questions*

(View segment 3: "What the Body Says")

*This video segment deals only with body needs in regard to end of life, not the entire aging process as discussed in this chapter. You may want to use this segment as a change of pace about half way through a session as you begin to focus on end of life, rather than to begin the session.*

1. Have you ever stood up to a doctor regarding their advice? What happened?

2. What are your experiences with being an advocate for someone else regarding their healthcare? Did they welcome your help or resent when you want to go in and see the doctor with them?

3. How can you be assertive in getting the healthcare someone needs—whether a clean, dry bed or a doctor to pay attention when you feel like he or she has written you off as too old, too poor, too unimportant?

## Chapter 4: Body, Mind, Spirit

### *Study questions*

1. Have we become so focused on the needs of families with young children within our congregations that we exclude older adults? In what ways can you help the older people be comfortable and actively involved in church and community life?

2. Using the definition of wellness cited in this chapter, respond to the following question. If Alice (in the opening illustration) were a member of your congregation, what all could be done to help her remain active in church life without placing her physical health at risk?

3. Consider our ethical obligations to not cause harm to others. While we would not knowingly injure someone, older adults can be more susceptible to injury than are younger people. Are we careful to stay away from others when we have upper respiratory infections? How careful are we with handwashing? Do we do our part to decrease air pollution and avoid releasing noxious substances into the air? Discuss the ways in which we inadvertently create risks for others.

4. Before class, find Scripture references on aging using a concordance (an easy-to-use online concordance can be found at www.gospelcom.net under Bible Gateway). Have group members take turns reading the Scriptures, then decide as a group if the image and underlying message is basically positive or negative. (The image may be negative while the message is positive.) How do these scriptures impact our thinking about aging?

5. **Child-friendly activity.** Assign homework for group members to explore the costs of several products and services that might be required by older adults. How much do hearing aids cost? How much does it cost for one year's supply of batteries? What is the cost of equipment and labor to permanently install grab bars around a bathtub and a toilet?

6. **Child-friendly activity.** Have group members find magazine or newspaper ads for prescribed drugs, over the counter medicines, and dietary supplements. Look at these in class and highlight their claims. How do these contribute to attitudes toward aging? (Save these to compare with ads you collect for youthful products in chapter 6.)

### *Video segment*

1. Tape two hours of random TV, then look for ads related to products for older people. Play one or two of them for the group. Again, discuss the claims or myths they perpetuate.

### *References and resources*

Ebersole, Priscilla and Patricia Hess. *Geriatric Nursing and Healthy Aging.* St. Louis: Mosby, 2001.

## Chapter 5: Redirection

### *Study questions*

1. What are two things you hope to be able to do during retirement that you do not have time to do now?

2. Do you expect that you will have trouble feeling worthwhile when you are not working full time? If so, why? If not, is there something that, if you couldn't do it anymore, would make you feel of less worth?

3. What have people in your congregation done in retirement that looks interesting or exciting to you?

4. What are some new ways you might be able to serve God when you have retired?

5. What are you doing now to give yourself something to do in retirement? Are there any hobbies you want to begin or renew? What if you lose your physical ability to do that activity? What back-up plan do you have?

6. Do you think gender makes a difference in how we face leisure time in retirement? Is it easier or harder for men or for women?

7. For spouses or people living in a shared environment, the following exercise may be helpful in discussions about mutual relationship goals in preparation for redirection. Break into pairs. Read the following questions one at a time and have group members discuss how to

answer each question. The pairs can help each other by discussing possible answers and sharing ideas.

a. What are some things you know now that you didn't know when you were younger?

b. How can knowing these things help you in the later years of life?

c. What are two strengths and skills that you developed in dealing with life to this point?

d. How can you use these strengths and skills to make your life better in later years?

e. What experiences and activities have given you the most satisfaction during your life?

f. How can you pursue similar experiences now and during the years ahead?

g. Who are some of the people who have given you the most support during your life?

h. What can you do to continue these relationships or to create similar ones?

*Used by permission 1986, Cook Communications Ministries, "Empty Nest: Life After the Kids Leave Home." Reprinted with permission. May not be further reproduced. All rights reserved.*

8. **Child-friendly activity.** For an extra session or separate activity while adult discussion occurs, invite several older people with hobbies to a special time with the children to demonstrate their hobby or collection.

### References and resources

Habitat for Humanity. www.habitat.org

Heifer International. PO Box 8058, Little Rock, AR 72203. 800-422-0474. www.heifer.org

Mennonite Association of Retired Persons (MARP). 771 Rt. 113, Souderton, PA 18964. 1-215-721-3120. marp-soop@juno.com

Rebuilding Together (formerly Christmas in April):
www.rebuildingtogether.org

Service Opportunities for Older People (SOOP):
Mennonite Mission Network, Box 370, Elkhart, IN
46515-0370. 1-574-294-7523.
SOOP@mennonitemission.net. Or: Mennonite Central
Committee Canada, 134 Plaza Dr., Winnipeg, MB R3T 5K9.
1-204-261-6381. Soop@mennonitecc.ca

## Chapter 6: What the Finances Say

### *Study questions*

1. When, if ever, should we consider the mass media and
   entertainment industry for perspective in our lives, families, and communities? Is this what used to be called "the
   world" by the church?

2. What do you want your family members to remember
   about your beliefs and values? How might you use the
   arrangement of your financial and legal affairs to accom-
   plish this?

3. How do you think God wants to "spend" you? How
   might this change as you age?

4. Where do people in your community go for information
   on legal and financial concerns? What do you think are
   the motives and value bases for these sources?

5. Do you think of the work of financial, insurance, and
   legal professionals in the church in the same way as
   medical, educational, and social service providers? Why
   or why not?

6. What ethical issues are involved in giving family assets to
   children to become eligible for public assistance for
   long-term care?

7. Do you agree that "Tithing as a *voluntary* spiritual discipline seems compatible with freedom in Christ and a healthy practice of self-restraint"?

8. Invite a Christian financial or estate planner or attorney to class to discuss aging issues and choices pertaining to your state or province.

9. **Child-friendly activity.** What is the biblical perspective on youth and physical beauty? Have the group look for ads directed to or featuring young people. Compare the images to the ads collected for health products for chapter 4.

### Video segment study questions
(View segment 6: "What the Finances Say")

1. What does Lynn Miller mean when he says, "You have a number of good years that you can give away at room and board prices"? Would that work for you? Why or why not?

2. Do you think the financial planning industry is scaring people into continuing a consumer lifestyle in old age, or is it good advice?

3. What do you think of Howard Brenneman's statement, "Insurance is just a mechanism to bring community back into play"? Do you agree or disagree? Discuss.

### Selected reference and resources

Dychtwald, Ken. *Age Power: How the Twenty-First Century Will Be Ruled by the New Old.* Los Angeles: J. P. Tarcher, 1999.

Shilling, Dana. *Financial Planning for the Older Client.* 5th ed. Erlanger, Ky.: National Underwriter Co., 2001.

Mennonite Mutual Aid. 1110 North Main St., PO Box 483, Goshen, IN 46527. 1-800-348-7468. www.mma-online.org

*Kiplinger's Personal Finance.* Washington, D.C.: The Kiplinger Washington Editors, Inc. www.kiplinger.com

## Chapter 7: Home Sweet Home

1. What images or memories do you associate with the words "home sweet home"?
2. Which of the three Scripture texts do you identify with most and why?
3. Which considerations and questions in "Getting Started" are most important to you?
4. Compare the older adult housing options and choices of your grandparents and parents. How are they similar? Different?
5. How are group members preparing for or how have they prepared for their older adult housing needs? How does this compare with the preparations made by their grandparents and parents?

### Video segment

1. Use a short video clip (even if it is mostly a promotional piece) from a local housing facility, retirement community, or nursing home as an introduction to the session.

### Activities

1. Invite a panel of older adults, representing as many housing options as possible, to come and:

   —Describe their current housing arrangements, how God led them there, how God ministers to them in that setting, and how they minister to others.

   —Discuss the advantages and disadvantages of their housing.

   —Say what they would do differently if they had a choice.

   —Advise class members regarding how and when to plan for future housing needs.

2. **Child-friendly activity.** Children could work on a plaque/motto of the words "Home Sweet Home" using whatever materials that can be provided: paints, markers, yarn, macaroni and glue, etc.

### References and resources

Bakker, Rosemary. *Elderdesign: Designing and Furnishing a Home for Your Later Years.* New York: Penguin Books, 1997.

Bruce, F. F., ed. *The International Bible Commentary: With the New International Version.* Rev. ed. Grand Rapids, Mich.: Zondervan, 1986.

Carter, Jimmy. *The Virtues of Aging.* New York: Ballantine, 1998.

Frankl, Viktor E. *From Death-Camp to Existentialism: A Psychiatrist's Path to New Therapy.* Trans. by Ilse Lasch. Boston: Beacon Press, 1959.

Friedan, Betty. *The Fountain of Age.* New York: Simon & Schuster, 1993.

Golant, Stephen M. *Housing America's Elderly: Many Possibilities/Few Choices.* Newbury Park, Calif.: Sage Publications, 1992.

Lyon, K. Brynolf. *Toward a Practical Theology of Aging.* Philadelphia: Fortress Press, 1985.

Pipher, Mary. *Another Country: Navigating the Emotional Terrain of Our Elders.* New York: Riverhead Books, 1999.

Thomas, L. Eugene and Susan A. Eisenhandler, ed. *Aging and the Religious Dimension.* Westport, Conn.: Auburn House, 1994.

Tournier, Paul. *Learn to Grow Old.* Louisville, Ky.: Westminster/John Knox Press, 1991.

Sapp, Stephen. *Full of Years: Aging and the Elderly in the Bible and Today.* Nashville: Abingdon Press, 1987.

Seymour, Robert E. *Aging without Apology: Living the Senior Years with Integrity and Faith.* Valley Forge, Pa.: Judson Press, 1995.

Wiebe, Katie Funk. *Life After 50: A Positive Look at Aging in the Faith Community.* Newton, Kan.: Faith & Life Press, 1993.

## Chapter 8: All in the Family

### *Study questions*

1. In what situations should children or younger family members start to make decisions for their parents? How can "honoring father and mother" be incorporated into this decision?

2. Should the congregation's pastoral team include a social work position to develop an information/resource bank for families and individuals? Could a parish nurse provide screening and counseling for members? (This is sometimes done after a church service on Sunday.)

3. If an elderly person does not have resources to pay for care that is needed and the public resources are not available, should the congregation develop a fund to help the family? Discuss pros and cons. (Even when services like fuel assistance are available, depending on the cost of heating oil, the supplement might not cover the actual cost. This is also true for prescription drug programs.)

4. Each state has a trained peer counseling program through area agencies on aging. These volunteers may assist with budgeting and other financial problems related to healthcare bills, insurance questions, and appeals. Consider whether your church should encourage volunteers to get this type of training.

### Video segment study questions

(View segment 8: "All in the Family")

1. Have you experienced family disagreements regarding care of parents? How have you handled them? Share stories as group members feel led, respecting privacy and confidentiality as the group decides.

2. How can we do a better job of preparing for the day when we will need help with our personal care? What do you do about people who say they would rather die than suffer those indignities?

3. Have you ever experienced new love and relationships through caring for someone during extended illness or dying? Share.

4. **Child-friendly activity.** Find a book in the church or public library that talks about extended, multi-generational families. Read to the children.

5. **Child-friendly activity.** Have children view the story, "Cuban Surprise" in the *Rhythms of Peace Around the World* video for children (available from Mennonite Media, 1-800-999-3534), showing an intergenerational household in Cuba. Use the discussion questions that accompany the video.

### References and resources

Dychtwald, Ken. *Age Power: How the Twenty-First Century Will Be Ruled by the New Old.* Los Angeles: J. P. Tarcher, 1999.

*Journey Toward Forgiveness,* sixty-minute documentary produced by Mennonite Media for ABC-TV telling six stories of families dealing with the death of a loved one and their issues related to forgiveness. Use single segments or, in a retreat setting, a good film to end with for the evening's entertainment. 1-800-999-3534.

## Chapter 9: It Takes a Congregation

*Study questions*

1. How does your congregation minister to older adults? What needs are currently not being met?

2. How do older adults minister to the congregation?

3. Where are there intergenerational opportunities in your congregation?

4. Where do older adults plug into congregational life? Where do they *not* plug in? Why?

5. Based on the gifts you recognize in the older adults in your congregation, what new possibilities might emerge for ministry?

6. Many church volunteers assist with the delivery of Meals on Wheels. In some cases, meals are needed beyond what the program provides and local congregations provide additional resources. Should the congregation help only their own members? Would this be a legitimate outreach for the congregation?

7. One congregation developed a team of volunteers who became involved in developing relationships with children with developmental or physical disabilities by providing respite for those families. Others were involved in a mentoring program with young adults who were returning to the community after serving prison sentences. With limited resources, it may be difficult for congregations to set priorities. Should your congregation consider intergenerational programs that involve older members of the church?

8. Often adults don't even know the names of children in the church. Have each participant intentionally talk to and remember the name of one new child in the congregation over the remaining sessions of this study.

9. As a group, assess activities in your church using the graph on the following page.

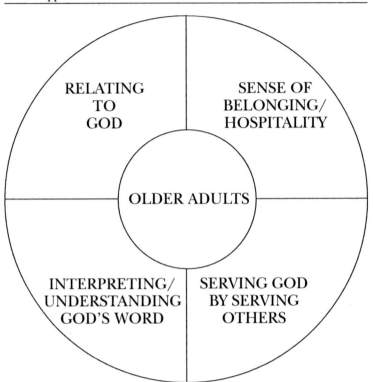

Instructions for use:

   a. Photocopy this drawing.

   b. Using one color of sticky note, list those activities in each quadrant in which older adults participate.

   c. Using a second color of sticky note, list new activities in which older adults could participate.

   d. Using this second list, think of specific names and gifts of older adults in your congregation.

   e. Consult with these older adults and see what the possibilities may be.

   f. Pray.

10. Mennonite Mutual Aid has a resource whereby you can do a complete review of a church's physical accessibility: "Becoming an Accessible Congregation" (www.mma-online.org/education_resources/ accessible_congregations.html) Have the group carry out the review or see that a task force is appointed to do so. Other denominations have similar programs.

### Video segment study questions
(View segment 9: "It Takes a Congregation")

1. Do you wish for more involvement of church in family situations in dealing with aging, or less? Why?

2. Does your minister play an active role in the end of life experiences of your congregation? Is that desirable, or not?

3. Barbara Springs uses the word "community," which could be interchanged with "congregation." Have you or your congregational community ever played a role in helping families reconcile at the end of life (or another transition point)?

### References and resources

Aleshire, Daniel O. *Faith Care: Ministering to All God's People Through the Ages of Life.* Philadelphia: Westminster Press, 1988.

Boucher, Therese M. *Spiritual Grandparenting: Bringing Our Grandchildren to God.* New York: Crossroad, 1991.

Cloyd, Betty Shannon. *Parents and Grandparents as Spiritual Guides: Nurturing Children of the Promise.* Nashville: Upper Room Books, 2000.

Friedan, Betty. *The Fountain of Age.* New York: Simon & Schuster, 1993.

Open Doors. For more information on the Open Doors concept, contact the Office of Congregational Life of Mennonite Church USA, 1-574-294-7523.

Taylor, Blaine. *The Church's Ministry with Older Adults.* Nashville: Abingdon Press, 1984.

## Chapter 10: Dying Well

### Study questions

1. What issues need to be discussed or processed in a family in order to have a good death? (Consider expressions of love, forgiveness, etc.)

2. How can the Christian deal with the ambivalence of knowing death means both a homegoing and a leave-taking?

3. Get samples of living wills or forms from your local hospital for each group member. Complete as homework or in the group together.

4. What has a dying person taught you?

5. Have group members share experiences of being present when a person died. How did the experience affect them?

6. **Child-friendly activity.** Have children draw or paint pictures of anything they remember about the death or funeral of a loved one or a pet.

### Video segment study questions
(View segment 10: "Dying Well")

1. John Perkins talks about wanting to die similarly to the way his son, Spencer did—suddenly from a heart attack. What are the advantages and disadvantages of dying suddenly versus having time to say good-bye?

2. How would you like to die? Are you fearful of pain? What are your other fears?

3. The video stresses that if the fears of pain and loneliness are dealt with, most people don't even think about assisted suicide. How do you feel about this issue? Can you understand people who think they would rather have control over their deaths than suffer through situations like Lou Gehrig's disease?

4. What kinds of artificial means of support do you think you want in the event you can't exist on your own?

### References and resources

Albom, Mitch. *Tuesdays with Morrie: An Old Man, A Young Man, and Life's Greatest Lesson.* New York: Doubleday, 1997.

*Beyond the News: Facing Death,* thirty-four-minute video from Mennonite Media. Includes some clips that are excerpted in the study video accompanying this book. 1-800-999-3534. info@mennomedia.org. www.thirdway.com/resources.

Callanan, Maggie, and Patricia Kelley. *Final Gifts: Understanding the Special Resources, Needs, and Communication of the Dying.* New York: Poseidon Press, 1992.

Dodd, Robert V. *Helping Children Cope with Death.* Scottdale, Pa.: Herald Press, 1984.

*I'll Give You the Gettin'.* Video with author Walter Wangerin Jr., telling the story of a couple dealing with the untimely death of the husband and the wife's struggle through anger to acceptance. Mennonite Media. 1-800-999-3534. info@mennomedia.org. www.mennomedia.org/resources.

Karnes, Barbara. *Gone from My Sight: The Dying Experience.* 1991. PO Box 335, Stilwell, KS 66085.

Kübler-Ross, Elizabeth. *Living with Death and Dying.* New York: MacMillan, 1981.

Larson, Dale. *The Helper's Journey: Working with People Facing Grief, Loss, and Life-Threatening Illness.* Champaign, Ill.: Research Press, 1993.

*On Our Own Terms: Moyers on Dying in America.* Video. Four-part series from the PBS Bill Moyers Specials. Films for the Humanities. 1-800-257-5126. custserv@films.com. www.films.com. (May be available in resource libraries.)

Platt, Nancy Van Dyke. *Pastoral Care to the Cancer Patient.* Springfield, Ill.: Thomas, 1980.

## Chapter 11: Saying Good-bye

### Study questions

1. Reflect on funerals you have attended. What in those services best celebrated the life of the deceased? What best helped you accept the loss? What helped you experience the love of God and hope for eternal life? What was less than helpful in these services?

2. Have older group members recall a typical funeral when they were young. What stands out in their memory?

3. Fill out the form in appendix D on planning your own funeral. Share it with the group.

4. In her book, *Border Crossing*, Katie Funk Wiebe writes about a "spiritual will" that could be read publicly. What are the spiritual gifts you are giving to your descendants and friends? What are you giving away from your own faith life?

5. Our faith values dictate that a funeral not be an ostentatious display of wealth. Discuss how to keep funeral costs minimal. Discuss concerns some people have that they will be viewed as "cheap" or miserly if they don't bury their parents in expensive caskets. Will people think they want to keep more estate money for themselves rather than for funeral expenses?

6. What are the events in life that cause you to think about the meaning of life, your own mortality, and eventual death?

### Video segment study questions

(View segment 11: "Saying Good-bye")

1. How do you feel about hands-on involvement in the funeral process: building a casket, digging a grave, filling the grave, scattering ashes, fixing the hair or clothing of a loved one?

2. What are ways your congregation could reduce funeral expenses for members?

3. Have you discussed cremation with your parents or with your children? How do you and they feel?

4. **Child-friendly activity.** Find the book, *Water, Bugs, and Dragonflies*, by Doris Stickney in a local library or on the Internet, or ask a librarian to help you find any suitable book explaining death to children. Read and discuss any questions they might have.

### *References and resources*

Stickney, Doris. *Water, Bugs, and Dragonflies: Explaining Death to Young Children.* Cleveland: Pilgrim Press, 1997.

Wiebe, Katie Funk. "Funerals Are Opportunities." Chapter 15 in *Border Crossing.* Scottdale, Pa.: Herald Press, 1995.

Wolfelt, Alan D. *Creating Meaningful Funeral Ceremonies: A Guide for Caregivers.* Fort Collins, Colo.: Companion Press, 1994.

———. *Creating Meaningful Funeral Ceremonies: A Guide for Families.* Fort Collins, Colo.: Companion Press, 1999.

York, Sarah. *Remembering Well: Rituals for Celebrating Life and Mourning Death.* San Francisco: Jossey-Bass, 2000.

## Chapter 12: A Toolkit for Aging

### *References and resources*

Packard, Vance. *A Nation of Strangers.* New York: McKay, 1972.

# Exercises to Help Experience the World as an Older Adult

## Older Adult Simulation Game
*(Chapter 1—Child-friendly activity)*

To simulate the walking difficulties often encountered by older people, have all class members agree to go through a day with a small rock in their shoe. It can be any day they choose, but try to go at least an eight-hour period with the rock.

Discuss:

1. Was the rock merely annoying, or did it actually become painful?
2. Did it cause any lasting pain the next day or make a sore where the stone rubbed?
3. Did you limp and did people notice it? Did you tell any of the people around you?
4. Were you embarrassed about the way you walked? Did you feel like people were looking at you?

## Happy Birthday—Another Year!
*(Chapter 1 or 2—Child-friendly activity)*

Have group members bring in a selection of birthday cards they have received. Look in particular for those that speak to age. What kinds of things do the cards poke fun at? Alternately, visit card stores in small groups and look for particularly bad and good stereotypes of aging.

1. How do you feel about age stereotyping on birthday cards? Is it fun? Is it funny?
2. How do you feel about "over the hill" parties and gift paraphernalia?

## Age Norming
*(Chapter 2)*

This exercise helps participants look at some of the societal norms or expected activities/associations that are generally applied to various age groups.

As a group, list on newsprint or marker board the following age ranges and then give the obligations and privileges associated with that age. One example is given.

| Age group | Obligations | Privileges |
| --- | --- | --- |
| 20-29 | Completing education work full-time, maybe start family | Gain independence from family, have own money |
| 30-39 | | |
| 40-49 | | |
| 50-59 | | |
| 60-69 | | |
| 70-79 | | |
| 80-89 | | |
| 90 and older | | |

When the chart is completed, discuss the following questions either in pairs, small groups, or as a whole group.

1. What do you think is the best age group? Do a vote among the group. Discuss your reasons for your vote.
2. How does your age group shape your concept of yourself?
3. Do you think this country is an age-graded society? Why or why not?
4. Discuss the privileges related to aging. How do they compare to the other privileges? Now that your group has had discussion, do another vote. Are the numbers still the same?
5. Extra: You may also want to add extra columns to chart the general views of different generations on various topics such as politics, religion, sexuality, etc.

## The Aging Stereotype Game
*(Chapter 3—Child-friendly activity)*

Divide into three groups: two groups of adults and one group of children. One group of adults should identify the positive stereotypes of aging; the second group identifies negative stereotypes of aging. The children's group identifies anything they think of when they think of "old people." After ten minutes, post three sheets of newsprint and alternate between the three groups calling out the items they have thought of.

Discuss:

1. How do stereotypes function in our society?
2. How are stereotypes useful or helpful? When are they damaging?
3. Which list (negative or positive) does the children's list most closely resemble?

## When Physical Function Is Limited
*(Chapter 4)*

Homework assignment: How does one learn to live with a chronic disease, disability, or impairment? Set up the following scenario for the group: You have just come from a visit to your doctor's office, and the doctor has told you that you have a chronic condition that can't be cured. You will need to learn to live with the condition. Assign conditions and do research, providing a brief oral or written report in the next group session.

1. Choose a hypothetical condition (such as arthritis, high blood pressure, high cholesterol, diabetes, multiple sclerosis, Parkinson's disease, hearing impairment) or choose one which already affects you or is present in your family.

2. Do research to define the condition, symptoms, how the symptoms change one's life, things they don't change.

3. How do you feel about this condition? What questions do you have? What are your fears?

4. Will you need any special equipment or changes to your home or habits in order to function well?

5. What organizations or associations are available to help?

6. How much help will you need from family or friends for daily activities?

7. Will family or friends treat you differently? How?

As a summary to this exercise, share real-life experiences of people you know learning to live with their limitations from specific conditions.

## Leisure Time

*(Chapter 5)*

Invite an older adult to class (or assign a class member) to talk about their experiences as a volunteer. Ask how they got involved, what the work is, why they enjoy it, what they don't enjoy, what it does for their personal life, and how it affects their self-esteem.

Discuss the following questions either with the older adult, or after he or she has left.

1. Why is self-esteem often tied to one's professional or leisure activities?

2. How do you want to spend your time when you are an older adult? Or, how do you most enjoy spending your time as an older adult?

3. Why is paid work usually more valued in our society than volunteer work?

4. On a chalkboard or newsprint, list the differences between what we do in "off time" when we are employed, versus what we do in "off time" when we are retired.


## Maintaining Independence

*(Chapter 6 or 7)*

This is an exercise geared mainly around discussion. You can have people write down their responses to these questions and then discuss, or divide up into pairs to discuss and then draw conclusions as a larger group.

1. Why is independence so important in our society? Are you aware of other societies where independence is not such a supreme value?

2. What does it mean to be independent? What does it mean for an older adult to be independent? Be specific. Another way of asking this is: When is an older adult no longer independent?

3. How can one have mental self-reliance or independence?
4. How does access to transportation affect the independence of older people?
5. How does money affect independence?
6. Why is moving out of one's home viewed as a loss of independence?
7. How can everyone around an older person help him or her stay as independent as possible?

## The Empty Bed
*(Chapter 8)*

Read the following case study in groups of two or four and discuss:

> Tom lost his wife, Barbara, to cancer when they were both sixty-three. They still enjoyed a healthy sex life right up till the last six months of their life together. He had lost other family members to cancer, so he knew well what was ahead for him: loneliness, perhaps depression, feeling like part of himself had been buried as well. His children lived nearby and visited often, but when he went to bed at night, the other half of his bed was very empty. Sometimes he could still smell Barbara's scent on her pillow.

> It was at times like this that Tom wondered: "How can I live the rest of my life without a wife? But no woman would ever be Barbara. My children love me, but they go home at night. I want to be touched and held close and loved like a man. I don't even feel like a man anymore, I just feel neutered. I didn't think I would ever want to be married again, but now I wonder if I will ever enjoy that part of my life again? What would people think if I got married? What would my children think? Should I just forget about sex?"

Discuss:

1. What common sexual myths are expressed by Tom's thoughts?
2. How does self-image relate to aging and sexuality?
3. Discuss ways Tom might experience more love and closeness without crossing any boundaries of appropriateness.
4. If Tom confided his thoughts to you, what would you recommend for him?

## Access

*(Chapter 9—Child-friendly activity)*

Do a survey regarding the physical layout of your church and ease of access for older adults. For comparison, also do a survey regarding the layout of a typical pharmacy in your area. Complete as homework between sessions, or in an extended session. In small groups visit different pharmacies. Compare the church and pharmacy.

1. Are parking spaces provided for older people and people with disabilities? How many?
2. How close are the spaces to the most desirable entrance—the one where older people need to go?
3. Is the front door easy to open?
4. Is the door wide enough to accommodate a wheelchair?
5. What kind of floor covering is used? Is it easy to walk over? Are there rug mats that make stumbling more likely?
6. How far is the appropriate section of the building from the front door?
7. Where are the restrooms in relation to the door and the sanctuary?
8. (**Church only**) Do a rough count of people in your congregation who have difficulty walking. Are there enough parking spaces for all who would use them if available?

(**Pharmacy only**) How many extra feet does one have to walk to get to the actual pharmacy counter? Pace it off. Pharmacies frequently make you walk a zigzag back through the store past the shelves, which encourages impulse purchases.

## Fear Walk
*(Chapter 9 or 3—Child-friendly activity)*

Spend ten minutes of class taking a "fear walk." Find a place preferably outside and over uneven terrain. If not outside, over a set of stairs or anywhere there are obstructions to walking.

Roles:

> *Children*—If your group has children, assign the children the role of "free play" and encourage them to run, dart around playing hide and seek or tag. If your group has no children, assign some adults to be "children" and have them do the same kinds of running around.

> *Adult walkers*—Assign four or five volunteers to be the "fear walkers." Role play that they recently recovered from a fall or surgery involving their hips or legs. They have spent months recuperating at home or in a nursing home. They are now attempting to get around without a cane or walker. Tell them they are deathly afraid of falling, of having to go through all that pain, rehabilitation, and expense again.

**Start:** At the signal, when the "children" start playing, have the walkers cross the designated area or go up the steps while children are running and playing loudly. Tell the children to be careful but to pretend that they are children playing. Place referees in the walking area to contain any children who get carried away and to prevent anyone from actually getting hurt! Repeat until everyone who wants to try it has had a turn.

**For extra learning:** Have the children pretend they are old and have also suffered a break. Have them walk across the designated area while other people "playing children" run and shout.

After the exercise discuss:

1. Why is falling such a frightening experience for many adults?

2. What is there about fear that makes the danger of falling worse?

3. Why do falls lead to more severe injuries for older people than younger ones?

4. Analyze your church in terms of likelihood of falling. How can you make your church safer?

5. For children: How did they feel when they were running around and playing? How did they feel when they were supposed to walk across the area? Did they learn anything new? Discuss finding places children can play after church without making it dangerous for other people.

6. Discuss how fear of falling sometimes leads to the older adult deciding to stay home rather than risk falling. How does this contribute to isolation, lowering of self-esteem, and perhaps depression? What can the church community do?

### *Most of the above activities adapted from:*

Fried, Stephen, Dorothy Van Booven, and Cindy MacQuarrie. *Older Adulthood: Learning Activities for Understanding Aging.* Baltimore: Health Professions Press, 1993. This book has many other excellent activities for experiencing the world of being an older adult. Check your local library, especially a college or university library, to see if it is available.

# Ritual for Leaving Work: "They Still Produce Fruit"

By Marlene Kropf
Office of Congregational Life, Mennonite Church USA, 2002.
Used by permission.

### Purpose of ritual

As they complete their days in the work world, older adults may be blessed by the congregation as they take up the joys and responsibilities of retirement. Though they often experience a satisfying sense of achievement, some may also face fears and uncertainties in these years. Many will be seeking a new sense of purpose. The purpose of this ritual is to:

–Remember and celebrate God's presence in the years given to work
–Provide a context of loving care, support, and discernment as individuals withdraw from a role where they have made a significant investment of time, energy, and creativity and now seek new direction
–Bless the ongoing journey of discipleship as retirees continue to follow Christ in the church and in the world

## Scripture focus

Psalms 92:1-4, 12-15. A meditation might emphasize the goodness of God's provisions throughout the person's lifetime as well as our hope in God's continuing care. The image of "remaining green and full of sap" in verse 14 adds a delightful, even humorous touch. Other texts which might be considered are Matthew 5:1-16; Philippians 3:7-14; and 1 Timothy 6:11b-16.

## Song suggestions

All numbers indicate hymns as found in *Hymnal: A Worship Book* of the Mennonite and Church of the Brethren denominations. Many will be familiar to readers of other denominations.

"For the fruit of all creation," No. 90
"Will you let me be your servant," No. 307
"Lord, whose love in humble service," No. 369
"What gift can we bring," No. 385
"Grant us, Lord, the grace," No. 388
"Go now in peace," No. 429
"O God, your constant care," No. 481
"God of our life," No. 486
"Gracious Spirit, dwell with me," No. 507

## Ritual action

Individuals who will be retiring are introduced. In brief interviews, stories may be told of how people came to do the work of their life. Following this introduction, several storytellers share stories that illustrate the gifts offered by these people in their place of work. At the conclusion of each story, clusters of fruit are added to the large bowl placed on a colorful cloth.

Those who have spoken and others form a circle of blessing around the older adults, place hands on them, and join in a prayer of blessing and commissioning. If desired, these people may also be anointed with oil to signify their desire for the Holy Spirit's presence and power.

At the conclusion of the ritual, a bowl of fruit is offered to each older adult as tangible evidence of the congregation's hopes and blessings.

**Prayer of blessing and anointing**
Lord Jesus Christ, you called (name) to be your disciple in the world of work as a _____. We give thanks for your call, for your strengthening grace, and for the harvest of the Spirit that has been gathered through the faithfulness of your servant. We are grateful that your love has been shared and your way made known through his/her efforts at work.

Now (name) is leaving a comfortable, familiar role to enter a new stage of life with new opportunities to minister and serve. We anoint her/him with the oil of blessing; guide and protect her/him on this journey. Grant courage and hope for the unknown. Make her/him flourish like a palm tree; in old age, let her/him still produce fruit. Keep her/him green and always full of sap. Into your hands we commit our sister/brother. We give thanks that you will never leave nor forsake her/him. In the name of the One who is our faithful Companion. Amen.

**Benediction**
Read 1 Corinthians 15:58.

# Planning Ahead for My Death

A sample from Park View Mennonite Church, Harrisonburg, Virginia

**Information your family needs to know** *(check off when each is completed)*

- Choice of funeral home and prearrangements made with them
- Preferences for funeral and burial sites
- Preferences for final deposition of the body: embalming or cremation
- Preferences for funeral or memorial service
- Information for obituary (full legal name, age, place and date of birth)
- Names of parents including mother's maiden name; cause of death; college degrees; occupation and places of work; place and date of marriage; memberships held including church; outstanding work: list of immediate survivors such as spouse, children, parents, sisters, brothers; time and place of viewing and funeral
- Choice of recipients of memorial contributions

- Choice of pallbearers (remember that older or disabled people can be honorary pallbearers)
- List of people to be informed at time of death (in addition to family)
- Location of this paper and other papers related to end of life arrangements

## *At time of death, your family will*

- Contact funeral home handling the arrangements
- Notify people to be informed of death (be sure to include the pastor)
- Decide on day and time of viewing, funeral, or memorial service
- Meet with clergy to plan funeral or memorial and committal service
- Write the obituary for the newspaper or provide information if the funeral home is handling newspaper notification
- Arrange for special household needs as family and friends respond to the death: answering doorbells, taking phone messages, caring for children, providing for food and housework, making lodging arrangements for out of town family. The local congregation will be helpful with these services
- Keep careful record of who brings food and flowers so notes of appreciation can be sent later
- Obtain death certificate from the doctor. Extra copies of the death certificate are needed in order to collect insurances, burial allowances, and other benefits
- Register death and obtain burial permit if required in your locality
- Notify insurance companies, Social Security office, bank, executor

## Funeral arrangements

In a funeral or memorial service at Park View Mennonite Church, we seek the presence of God in our grieving and celebrate the grace of God which we saw in this person. Each person's life is precious in God's sight, and we want a funeral or memorial service to respect and give honor to each person's unique life journey. While each service differs in the details, a service usually includes prayer, Scripture, music, a meditation, and remembrances. Funeral details family will assist pastor with:

—Time and place of viewing, visitation hours, funeral or memorial service, committal at graveside

—Planning order of funeral or memorial service and choosing people to be involved

—Deciding whether there is an open or closed casket

—Contacting those involved with service

—Choosing the design and content of printed order of service

—Making arrangements for meal if there is one

## Funeral preferences:

You are free to change these preferences at any point. We recognize that not all choices may be honored due to a variety of reasons. Copies of this should be given to the pastor, to appropriate family members, and filed with your other papers about funeral arrangements.

Officiating clergy:

Song leader:

Hymns:

Special music (vocal and instrumental) and musicians:

Scriptures:

People to do remembrances, eulogy, reflections:

Other preferences or comments:

# Websites

AARP (formerly American Association of Retired Persons): www.aarp.org

Administration on Aging (AoA): www.aoa.dhhs.gov

The Alzheimer's Association: www.alz.org

American Association of Homes and Services for the Aging (AAHSA): www.aahsa.org

American Bar Association Commission on Legal Problems of the Elderly: www.abanet.org/aging

American Health Care Association (AHCA): www.ahca.org

Assisted Living Federation of America (ALFA): www.alfa.org

Caregiving Online: www.caregiving.com

Center for Medicare Education: www.MedicareEd.org

Department of Health and Human Services (HHS): www.os.dhhs.gov

Department of Housing and Urban Development (HUD): www.hud.gov

ElderWeb: www.elderweb.com

Medicare Information: www.medicarerights.org

Mennonite Association of Retired Persons (MARP) www.marp.mennonite.net

My Home Store: www.homestore.com

National Aging Information Center (NAIC): www.aoa.dhhs.gov/naic

National Association of Home Builders (NAHB): www.nahb.com

National Center for Assisted Living (NCAL): www.ncal.org

National Family Caregivers Association: www.nfcacares.org

National Parkinson Foundation, Inc.: www.parkinson.org

National Stroke Association: www.stroke.org

National Senior Citizen's Law Center: www.nsclc.org/consumers

National Shared Housing Resource Center (NSHRC): www.nationalsharedhousing.org

Nursing Home Compare: www.medicare.gov/nhcompare/home.asp

Partnership for Caring—America's Voice for the Dying: www.partnershipforcaring.org

Retirement Net—Retirement Communities and Retirement Homes: www.retirenet.com

Senior Care Web: www2.seniorcareweb.com

USDA Rural Development—Rural Housing Service: www.rurdev.usda.gov/rhs

# The Authors

**Ann Bender** is the recently retired executive director of Valley Program for Aging Services, Inc., the area agency on aging serving the Central Shenandoah Valley of Virginia. Ann lives with her husband, Titus, in the rural town of New Hope, Va., one hundred yards from daughter, Maria, son-in-law, Joe and three granddaughters. Their son, Michael, and his family, live in Atlanta, Tex., and daughter Anita lives in Moorhead, Minn. Ann is the current president of the ElderAlliance in the Shenandoah Valley and is a member of the board of directors for Generations Crossing, a multi-generational day program in Harrisonburg.

**Shirley Yoder Brubaker**, Harrisonburg, Va., recently retired, was associate pastor at Park View Mennonite Church. She and her husband, Kenton, returned recently from Lithuanian Christian College in Lithuania, where Shirley taught writing and Kenton worked at landscaping the college campus. Prior to the Lithuanian adventure, the Brubakers served as interim pastors at Jubilee Mennonite Church, Meridian, Miss. Shirley's "spiritual will" includes giving away her deep love for the church, for planning worship rituals, and for teaching.

**Pam Reese Comer** is a licensed professional counselor with more than seventeen years of experience working with the issues of death, loss, and grief. She has worked as a trainer and consultant with state and local hospice organizations, community businesses, churches, and healthcare organizations. Currently she is in private practice with Family Life Resource Center, a faith-based counseling center in Harrisonburg, Va.

**Melodie M. Davis** is a writer/producer for Mennonite Media, Harrisonburg, Va., author of the weekly syndicated newspaper column, "Another Way," and the editor of *Together* and *Living* papers for the Shalom Foundation. She graduated from Eastern Mennonite University and is the author of eight books and various curriculum materials. She is married to Stuart and they have two college-age daughters and a daughter in high school. They are members of Trinity Presbyterian Church in Harrisonburg, a house-church congregation.

**Evelyn Driver** is a professor of nursing at Goshen (Ind.) College, where she teaches courses in gerontological nursing, adult medical-surgical nursing, and nursing research. Her dissertation research at the University of Virginia focused on the concept of autonomy in old age and explored the meanings of the term "independence for nursing home residents." She attends College Mennonite Church in Goshen.

**Ken Hawkley** works for Mennonite Church USA as assistant director in charge of discipling ministries for the Office of Congregational Life. He worked for the former Commission on Education for the General Conference Mennonite church for twelve years and has been a conference speaker and workshop presenter, as well as congregational consultant and writer. He has co-authored two Bible studies on the Vision: Healing and Hope statement of Mennonite Church USA. He has also written two other Bible studies for the *Good Ground: Letting the Word Take Root* series, a series he helped develop. Ken enjoys his job of "helping people fall in love with Jesus Christ." He is married to Louise and has two grown children, Krysta and Jared, both in college.

**Suzanne Kennedy** is associate director of gift planning and alumni relations at Eastern Mennonite High School, Harrisonburg, Va. Prior to that she served as the Mennonite Foundation representative in the southeastern region of the U.S. for five and a half years, working with individuals in the areas of charitable giving and estate planning consultation and with churches and church-related organizations for investment management. She also served on the development staff of the Presbyterian Church (USA) Foundation and has a corporate management background in marketing research and strategic business planning. She graduated from Virginia Polytechnic Institute with a bachelor's degree in mathematics (1971) and holds an MBA from Northern Illinois University (1982). Suzanne and her family live in Harrisonburg and are members of Lindale Mennonite Church.

**Pearl Lantz** has experience in both nursing and social work in geriatric settings. She is a graduate of James Madison University, Harrisonburg, Va., and as a "first wave" baby boomer, is aware that aging issues are becoming increasingly personal. Currently she works in apartment management and resides in Harrisonburg with her husband, Dick; they have two adult children. They are members of Harrisonburg Mennonite Church.

**Barbara K. (Bender) Reber** lives in Goshen, Ind., with her husband, Don. They are members of College Mennonite Church and parents of five adult children. They spent fifteen years under Mennonite Board of Missions as mission workers in Japan and continue their contacts with Japan. Barbara also teaches English to Japanese in this country. She served as executive director of churchwide Mennonite Women (formerly W.M.S.C.) and was founder and director of Mennonite Association of Retired Persons (MARP). A significant activity of MARP was the development of Service Opportunities for Older Persons (SOOP). During her leadership of MARP she also founded the Mennonite Senior Sports Classic. She continues to be active in a variety of local boards and church responsibilities.

**Lonnie Yoder** is professor of pastoral care and counseling at Eastern Mennonite Seminary, Harrisonburg, Va., since 1991. He received his B.A. from Drake University, M.Div. from Associated Mennonite Biblical Seminary, and a Ph.D. from the University of Iowa. He is married to Teresa and they have two daughters. They recently spent a sabbatical year in Jamaica. He is member of Community Mennonite Church in Harrisonburg.